# A Passion for
# Orchids

L. Stroobant del & lith

Jack Kramer

# A Passion for
# Orchids

The Most Beautiful Orchid Portraits
and their Artists

Photography by Eric Strachan

Prestel

Munich · Berlin · London · New York

© for text and illustrations by Jack Kramer
© for design and layout by Prestel Verlag, Munich · Berlin · London · New York, 2002

The right of Jack Kramer to be identified as author of this work has been asserted in accordance with the Copyright, Designs and Patents Act 1988.

Front jacket: J. Nugent Fitch, *Cattleya lawrenciana* (detail).
Frontispiece: L. Stroobant, *Phaius tankervilleae.*
Back jacket: Miss Taylor, *Acanthephippium bicolor.*

Prestel-Verlag
Mandlstrasse 26
D-80802 Munich
Germany
Tel.: (89) 38-17-09-0
Fax.: (89) 38-17-09-35
www.prestel.de

4 Bloomsbury Place
London
WC1A 2QA
Tel.: (020) 7323 5004
Fax.: (020) 7636 8004

175 Fifth Avenue, Suite 402
New York
NY 10010
Tel.: (212) 995 2720
Fax.: (212) 995 2733
www.prestel.com

Library of Congress Control Number: 2002101409

Prestel books are available worldwide. Please contact your nearest bookseller or any of the above addresses for information concerning your local distributor.

Editorial direction: Philippa Hurd
Production: Ulrike Schmidt

Origination: Trevicolor, Dosson di Casier (TV)
Printing: Sellier, Freising
Binding: Conzella, Pfarrkirchen

Printed in Germany
ISBN 3-7913-2699-6

# CONTENTS

# Preface and Acknowledgements

Although many flower families offer a variation in color and form, only in the Orchidaceae do we find such tremendous variation. The family's uniqueness has made the orchid an obsession with artists and hobbyists, as well as a passion of many flower lovers.

Orchids head the flowering plant families in the perfection of their floral machinery, which is both complex and beautiful. The various shapes of orchid flowers range from curious flowers that resemble birds in flight, bees, wasps, butterflies, and spiders to orchids which resemble parts of the human anatomy. The orchid family also has its share of mysticism, glamour, and enticement. In an orchid flower one can find emotion, lust and passion. One often sees people at orchid exhibits staring transfixed at a single orchid flower.

This book provides a background on orchids as well as a stunning gallery of some of the best but seldom seen orchid illustrations of the nineteenth century. Profiles on their artists are also included. The illustrations are taken from my personal library which represents thirty years of rare book collecting.

I should like to thank the librarians from libraries and museums throughout the United States and England whose help has been invaluable in the preparation of this book.

My thanks also go to the following libraries, museums, and arboretums:

Hunt Institute for Botanical Documentation, Carnegie Melon University, Pittsburgh, PA
Stroetzer Library, Florida State University, Tallahassee, FL
Florida State University, Tallahassee, Florida
Academy of Natural Sciences, Philadelphia, PA
Pierpont Morgan Library, New York, NY
Naples Public Library, Main Branch, Naples, FL
The New York Botanical Garden, New York, NY

The Academy of Natural Science, Philadelphia, PA
The Metropolitan Museum of Art, New York, NY
The Natural History Museum, London, England
The Massachusetts Horticultural Society, Boston, MA
The Academy of Science, San Francisco, CA
The University of Florida, Gainesville, FL
Broughton Library, Harvard University, Cambridge, MA
Morton Arboretum, Lisle, IL
New York Historical Society, New York, NY
New York Society of Illustrators, New York, NY
The New York Public Library, New York, NY
The Linnean Society, London, England
Free Library of Philadelphia, Philadelphia, PA
The British Museum, London, England
The Lindley Library, London England
Royal Botanic Gardens, Kew, England
The Arnold Arboretum, Harvard University, Jamaica Plains, NY
The Fitzwilliam Museum, Cambridge, England
Royal Horticultural Society, London, England
Sotheby's, New York

My thanks to Eric Strachan, who photographed the illustrations for this book. I am grateful to Andrew Roy Addkinson, former Head of Environmental Design at the College of Arts and Crafts in Oakland, California, for his advise on art techniques and printing, and to Jan Deas for her computer expertise.

And my sincere appreciation and thanks to Philippa Hurd of Prestel who immediately grasped the idea of this book, and gratitude to Jürgen Tesch, publisher, and his staff, for a fine production.

*Jack Kramer*, Spring 2002

# A PASSION FOR ORCHIDS

The rose may be associated with romance but the orchid has become the flower of both pageantry and practicality. Once thought of only as a corsage flower or a Mother's Day plant, orchids are today the number one best-selling houseplant in America. Where carnations and roses once dominated commercial greenhouses, orchids today hold sway. Hundreds of orchid shows are sponsored by various societies in malls, banks, fairs and through events organized by the American Orchid Society. Orchids, once thought rare and exotic have become an everyday plant.

For decades the orchid has been maligned by some, respected by others, hated and even feared, revered and even worshipped by civilizations. Early British collectors considered it, erroneously, to be a parasite. Aztec civilizations thought it was a god. Orchids were cast as man-eating plants in Hollywood movies of the 1930s and 1940s. Parts of the plant (the bulbs) were used as an aphrodisiac. But no matter how people viewed the plant they always saw the orchid flower itself as beautiful, though mysterious.

Myths and legends have abounded about orchids since ancient Greece. Although a reputation for aphrodisiac properties has followed orchids throughout the ages, it has no chemical validity. Other myths originated from the tales of early orchid collectors who, trying to keep their territory secret from rival collectors, concocted stories about dangerous cannibals. One orchid (an epidendrum) brought back on one of the ship voyages over a period of some three months, grew and bloomed in the captain's cabin without aid of soil or water, as if divinely nurtured. Still other tales arose when collectors saw orchids growing on roofs of chapels and on arches as if sent by God or endowed with magical powers. Certainly orchids (being epiphytes) will grow on such surfaces unaided by soil or by a gardener's touch.

Other myths came from the common names of orchids such as the Holy Ghost orchid (*Peristeria*) or the vanishing orchid, a cattleya that was discovered once and then not rediscovered for decades. The tiger orchid (*Rossioglosum*) named for its brown and yellow stripes, was said to be found only in lands, where the tiger dwells. Still other stories abound linked to orchids' resemblance to a bee, hornet, or hummingbird. People have created all sorts of speculations and allegations about orchids and their origins and supernatural properties. But in truth orchids are simply beautiful gifts of nature.

European acquaintance with orchids began in 1731 when British explorers returned home with orchids collected from many countries including the West Indies. World travel had increased and English ships were returning with new plants including the orchid which ironically was accidentally used as a packing material for other plants of more economic use. Part of the attraction was the sensational lore surrounding orchids, such as the belief that orchids ate animals.

Other factors that contributed to the mystique included the orchid's tendency to strangle trees with their massive root systems and its ability to survive three-month ocean voyages without water and light.

British royalty were among the first to become enthralled with orchids—and among the first to be able to afford them—and ordered their gardeners to cultivate the plants. Eventually the orchid became popular when the glass tax was repealed in England in 1845 and more middle-income people could afford glass houses (conservatories) to house their exotic blooms.

Today, orchids with their alluring attractiveness and beauty are grown by the thousands by many people. This plant family has captured the hearts and souls of flower lovers, creating a passion for orchids.

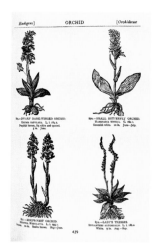 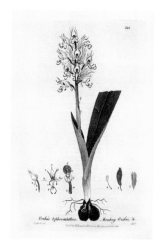

Herbals of the times designated (classed) orchids as *orchis*, and considered it the name for the entire family.

In Baxter's *Botanic Garden* of 1837 the resemblance of orchid bulbs to male genitalia is apparent, thus it was used as an aphrodisiac.

*Western Origins*

The orchid, among numerous other plants in antiquity and medieval times, was used for medicinal purposes, chiefly as an aphrodisiac. Frequently herbalists felt that the shape of the plant parts which resembled counterparts in the human anatomy would cure ailments affecting that part of the body. For example, hepatica leaves resemble the human liver, so leaves properly prepared were thought to cure liver ailments. Thus, orchids, whose bulbs have a testicular shape, were associated with sexual prowess, and were chopped, ground, and boiled in water and prescribed to cure sexual dysfunction in the herbals of ancient times. To this day people still associate the orchid, albeit in a romantic manner, with love and passion, and its exotic beauty creates an aura of romance.

The Greek-derived word orchid was coined in the manuscript *Enquiry into Plants* by the Greek philosopher Theophratus (372–287 B.C.E), sometimes called

the Father of Botany. He used *orchis* (meaning "testis") to designate the entire Orchid family. After studying plants from one genus, Theophratus concluded that all plants of that genus shared the same features and so made no distinction between orchids from his Mediterranean areas and those from other parts of Europe. Mediterranean flowers are small and almost insignificant compared to today's cattleyas which can reach seven inches in diameter. Greek physician and botanist, Dioscorides, wrote a work titled *Materia Media* in the first century in Asia Minor while serving as surgeon for Nero's Roman army wherein he described two orchids from Theophratus's work. Dioscorides, also considered orchids an aphrodisiac and named them *Cynorchis*. Dioscorides' views on orchids remained an authority for sixteen centuries and became fully rooted in European history. *The Doctrine of Signatures*, a philosophical work of the Middle Ages, perpetuated the myths which associated orchids with sexuality). The name *orchis* followed the orchid for many decades reappearing in Joseph Pitton

In Green's *Universal Herbal* the orchids still appear as the family *orchis* harking back to a century-old name since no plant classification had been established.

Constatine Rafinesque's *Medical Flora* (1830) shows a *cypripedium*; note that the drawing is decorative as well as useful for identification.

Tournefort's *Institutiones rei herbariae* (1700). In Thomas Green's *Universal Herbal* (c. 1824) reference is made to the flower *Orchis mascula*.

The German Jesuit Athanasius Kircher (1601–80) confirmed that the orchid could serve as a sexual stimulant in his *Mundus subterraneus* (1665). To the word *orchis* he added the term *Satyrion* (meaning "Satan"), based on the Greek myth that orchids sprang from the ground where animals' sperm had fallen during mating. Little wonder then that Satyrion bulbs (tubers) were boiled and brewed as an aphrodisiac. The term *Satyrion* followed the orchid into the seventeenth century when true botanical science began with Linnaeus in 1737 who developed the famous system of plant classification that remains the international standard today. Linnaeus placed orchids and other plants into families and subfamilies called genera based on similarities of reproductive parts such as stamens, pistils, and ovaries. In 1753 he described eight orchid species; in 1763 he named some 100 and classified them into one genus: epidendrum.

## The Far East

Orchids were known, described, and illustrated in China and Japan long before their importance was acknowledged in Europe, as for centuries Asia exchanged no plant information with Europe, and the Japanese feared that foreign influences would disrupt their society. In 1639 all foreigners were restricted to a small island called Deshima in Nagasaki harbor, though a few years later members of the Dutch East India Company were admitted.

The Chinese and Japanese assigned no healing or aphrodisiac properties to orchids. Instead they celebrated the flower's sweet scent and beauty, especially the green or white flowers. Plum blossoms and chrysanthemums were favored in paintings and drawings, but orchids held a prominent place as well, in particular cymbidium orchids, known for their graceful leaves. Chinese reference to orchids dates back to 230 C.E. and orchids were called *lan* in the works of Confucius (551–479 B.C.E). During the Northern Sung period (960–1279) monographs on orchids appeared. The Yuan Dynasty (1279–1368) was especially noted for its depiction of orchids, and orchids were among the four noble plants of the Ming Dynasty (1378–1644)

The Chinese were fond of orchids not for their beauty, but rather for their fragrance. Cymbidium often featured in their brush paintings because of its graceful leaves.

(the other three were bamboo, plum, and chrysanthemum). Even today when you glance around a Chinese restaurant, for example, you will see orchids on wallpaper or plateware. The most celebrated group of Chinese orchid paintings is to be found in the *Mustard Seed Garden* painting manuals by Wang An-Chien and his three brothers.

Although orchids have been cultivated for well over a thousand years in China, wild orchids were also admired in paintings from as early as the eleventh century. Many Westerners who view these classical Chinese paintings and drawings mistake the orchids for stylized jonquils or narcissi. In a book by Matsuoka painted in 1772 six orchids were cited: *Cymbidium ensifolium, Angraecum falcatum, Cymbidium virescens, Dendrobium moniforme* and *Bletia hyacinthina*. These purely aesthetic illustrations had no rival in the European woodblock illustrations from herbals where botanical accuracy was paramount.

brought both home. In 1760 *Epidendrum rigens* was seen in England, and in 1765 the fabulous and highly colored Vanilla orchid, with bright yellow flowers, caused a stir in England. Naval officers also returned with outlandish stories about plants that lived on other plants and this misconception of orchids persists today.

In the mid-eighteenth century, the British fleet constantly plied the seas in search of flora and fauna. The Royal Society's director, Sir Joseph Banks, accompanied Captain James Cook on the H.M.S. *Endeavour* on Cook's historic round-the-world voyage of 1768–71 during which Cook charted the coasts of New Zealand and eastern Australia. This voyage also included Daniel Solander, a pupil of Linnaeus and Keeper of the Natural History Department of the British Museum who collected hundreds of botanical specimens. Also aboard was Sydney Parkinson, a well-known botanical artist, who created an enormous record of plants in pencil and watercolor.

*And all the Ships at Sea*

As we have seen, orchids played an important role in Oriental cultures as early as the Sung Dynasty (960–1279) and the flower, aside from its medicinal uses in Europe, remained essentially undiscovered until the 1700s. Peter Collinson, a collector from New Providence Island in the Bahamas, is said to have introduced the first tropical orchid *Bletia verecunda* to Europe. The plant flowered with bright magenta blooms for Sir Charles Wagner in 1733. It is still grown today by collectors.

The West Indies, especially Jamaica, was easily accessible to European ships. Naval officers, seeking ways to while away the time, were struck by the beauty of Jamaica's plants, as well as its parrots, and

Typical habitat of phalaenopsis orchids taken from an old *Gardener's Chronicle* publication. The surrounding vegetation signifies a tropical environment but not necessarily a climate of excessive humidity or heat.

In his *Himalayan Journals* (1891) Sir Joseph Dalton Hooker shows a typical environment where orchid hunters sought out plants for England.

However, not all voyages of exploration were complete successes. On a world voyage beginning in 1776, Captain Cook was killed by natives in the Hawaiian Islands. Undeterred, King George III, in 1789, asked Joseph Banks if he could, among other botanical missions, bring back breadfruit from the Pacific Islands to the West Indies as commercial crop. Command of the ship was given to a former sailing master on Captain Cook's fatal final voyage, William Bligh. In 1793 he set out for the South Pacific in the H.M.S. *Providence* and returned with orchids including *Oncidium altissimum, O. carthaginense, Lycaste barringtonia,* and *Epidendrum ciliare.* Orchids, once considered bizarre plants, were slowly gaining popularity in domestic conservatories. Soon other countries decided to join the hunt and Belgium, Germany, and France started exploring for orchids. They sent out many explorers to capture and bring back the elusive plants that grew on tree branches, hugged mountainous cliffs, and seemed to exist on air without soil.

John Lindley the famous orchidologist (1799–1865), was a professor of botany and secretary of the Royal Horticultural Society and also edited a garden magazine. In his *Collectanea Botanica* in 1821 he declared:

> *If we are requested to select the most interesting from the multitude of vegetable tribes, we should on the whole perhaps be willing to give the preference to the natural order of Orchidaceae….*

## England's Passion for Flowers

Orchidologists cite various dates for the beginning of orchid cultivation in England, and no exact originating date is certain. The emergence of orchids as the flower of the nineteenth century came about from a combina-

In K.L. Blume's *Flora Javae* we see a typical orchid environment— dense forests and cool mountains.

For many decades all orchids coming into England were designated as *epidendrums;* in this case the name was correct.

tion of timed circumstances. The Royal Botanic Gardens in Kew, England, had begun cultivating orchids as early as 1759. At that time the West Indies was a famous hunting ground for plants and a tropical land accessible to Europeans. In 1786 Kew Gardens had about twenty-four orchid species in their collection, most of which were tropical. In Aiton's *Hortus Kewensis* (1759) many cultivated orchids were listed some of which are still favorites with hobbyists today. These include *Epidendrum fragrans, Phaius tankervillae,* and *Epidendrum cochleatum* which first bloomed in 1789. Seeing these orchids blossoming for the first time in cultivation was an event. By 1846 Kew had some forty-six specimens of tropical origin and others from South America and Australia. This was just the beginning.

Sir William Jackson Hooker, a devotee of exotic species, became director of Kew in 1841. England in the early 1800s was a gardening nation, as it still is today, and then, as now, plants of all kinds figured strongly in English daily life. Virtually all grand houses featured ubiquitous palms and garden flowers ranging from sweet peas to auriculas, and greenhouses were

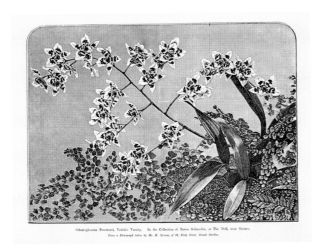

In nineteenth century orchid collections a display of *Odontoglossum pescatorie* is shown. These orchids from cool climates became popular and excessive heating was not needed.

often an integral part of the property. But the orchid was unlike anything seen before. Its variation in form and color astounded the public. Unfortunately, few knew how to grow orchids successfully. Growers assumed that all orchids came from the tropical, humid lands and so attempted to duplicate those environments. Many did come from the tropics but flourished at high altitudes, and thus required rather cool conditions. As a result thousands of orchids perished. In spite of the failures public demand increased and it became something of a challenge to see if one could bloom an orchid plant.

In 1815 Conrad Loddiges, a plantsman and editor of *The Botanic Cabinet* decided to grow orchids in an unorthodox manner. He kept them in his conservatory but treated them as ordinary garden plants, affording ample ventilation and light. The plants responded well. At first his attempts were ignored, but when other owners of conservatories saw his success they copied his methods.

With the knack for growing established, an orchid craze developed. "Orchidomania" set in, not unlike the

"tulipomania" that had caused financial chaos in the Netherlands and Near East during the seventeenth century.

The demand for new orchids—like our present-day hybrids—created exorbitant prices. The orchid became the flower of the era, popular for its beauty and its scarcity as well as its fascinating lore. Coaxing never-before-seen orchids into bloom achieved recognition with the wealthy and royalty. The auction sales at Covent Garden, Stevens Rooms, King Street, and other establishments became hotly contested with everyone vying for the prize orchid. Some cattleya orchids in the 1860s sold for more than $1,000 in today's money.

As many as 15,000 new kinds of plants (many of which were orchids) had been introduced into cultivation during the eighteenth century. Such a plethora of flowers gave proof of England's wealth and embellished the image of the monarchy.

George III's father Frederick, Prince of Wales, founded the gardens at Kew. In 1772 the garden passed to George III and when the plantsman Sir Joseph Banks became director, flowers and plants entered every facet of interior decorating, from draperies to needlepoint to furniture motif. William Aiton, the young gardener at Kew listed many species in his *Hortus Kewensis* (1789).

During the Victorian period the English passion for flowers resulted in the introduction of a wide range of plants. For high-minded Victorians flowers represented life and resurrection through their cycle of blossoming, death, and reappearance. By this time Linnaeus' scientific naming system had been universally accepted, and had transcended its academic context, moving into social circles. Now people of refinement could identify exactly what they wanted and what they were growing which resulted in the same sort of nomenclature that continues today. Linnaeus claimed that there was no better way to pay homage to the Creator than by indulging in the pleasures of flower growing.

In England, the Duchess of Portugal brought Linnean botany to the forefront by introducing Queen Victoria to her teacher of botany, Sir James Edward Smith, who founded the Linnean Society. He was knighted in 1814. Flower painting also came into vogue. Artists were commissioned and many people took up flower painting which became a national pastime. In the early 1800s how-to books on flower painting were as common as flypaper. These little books provided step-by-step processes, and illustrated the techniques with uncolored and colored versions of flowers and templates to copy.

The French also followed the vogue in flowers: Versailles was a garden haven abounding with flowers. Fashionable ladies took lessons in flower painting from great masters such as Redouté. Napoleon's wife, Josephine, was a flower aficionado too, as proven by the wonderful albums she commissioned from

Rebecca Hey was one of the popular writers of the language of flower books and this shows an example of decorative botanical art.

Typical habitat of phalaenopsis orchids taken from an old *Gardener's Chronicle* publication. The surrounding vegetation signifies a tropical environment but not necessarily a climate of excessive humidity or heat.

Redouté on the lilies and roses of her Malmaison Gardens.

While the British tended to revere flowers for their moral significance as well as their beauty, the French were attracted by more romantic ideal, publishing books on the "language of flowers". These books combined floral drawings with sentimental verse and prose. In England by the mid-nineteenth century books by the dozens were celebrating flowers. Louisa Anne Twamley wrote *Flora's Gems*, Rebecca Hey *The Moral of Flowers* and *Spirit of the Woods* and other such titles, all celebrating the glory of flowers. Books such as Wakefield's *Conversation in Botany* and Lindley's *Ladies' Botany* enjoyed dozens of printings.

The colored version of single dahlias taken from Ethel Nesbit's 1888 how-to-paint flower book.

Orchids appeared in wallpapers, picture, fabrics and many locations during the period of orchidomania.

From Sir Joseph Dalton Hooker's *Himalayan Journals* we see a typical background of trees and vegetation where orchids live.

*Orchid Hunting*

Between 1840 and 1850, the demand for orchids soared in England as royalty filled conservatories with exotic showpieces.  Like the animal trophies of the time, orchids became a major quarry of the plant world and collectors went forth, map in hand. Those who went to capture orchids made for dramatic accounts. Orchid hunting was by no means easy, but it paid big money. The hunt usually took place in inhospitable climates of heat and humidity, in insect-infested lands and among unfriendly natives, some of whom were cannibals. Many collectors never returned.

In 1850 English explorers penetrated Central and South America where orchids grew in abundance, and still do. William Lobb and Benedict Roezl collected for several firms. Other orchid collectors traveled to Africa, Java, Borneo, and New Guinea, all of which had large selections of orchids. A map showing the location of orchids was akin to a treasure map. Sadly, collectors in their zeal—and greed—collected, and thereby destroyed, whole stands of orchids, and were highly jealous of each other's finds. Commonplace palms, cacti, and geraniums lost their importance in the face of the orchids which were now filling the conservatories.

Alongside London, Hamburg in Germany shared the dominance of the orchid trade. The blossoming of an orchid was an occasion for celebration in the House of Hamburg where it was announced in newspapers. At this time the frenzy for orchids peaked in England where buyers paid exorbitant prices for a fine cattleya specimen. In Germany that cattleya would bring as much as 1,000 marks at the time.

Dozens of collectors, employed by various orchid nurseries and growers, ventured forth: men such as James Bateman, Benedict Roezl, Louis Schlim, Charles Wagner and Josef Warscewicz. Roezl traveled in Mexico and South America; employed by Linden, a Belgian firm, Schlim traveled all over the world; Wagner journeyed from Munich to collect in tropical America. Because orchids are mainly tree dwellers and because no respectable European would climb to the treetops of rain forests, natives were hired to retrieve the orchids. Yet even when a collector found a stand of orchids, the task of transporting the plants home was no easy matter. The combination of heat and humidity usually destroyed the plants before they reached their destinations. The voyage on ships for months with no water or light also added to the demise of hundreds of orchids since most were epiphytes requiring both air and light. Most plants were dead on arrival.

Jean Linden, the Belgian horticulturist, sent back thousands of plants. But because he needed to keep his source locations secret from rivals, buyers never really knew where their plants came from and thus had little idea of how to cultivate them and the conditions they needed. Nevertheless, demand soared. Linden was only nineteen when he started hunting orchids. He first explored the regions of Rio de Janeiro, Minas Gerais and São Paulo, moving on to collect in Cuba, Mexico, and Guatemala. Through intermediaries Linden met the famous explorer and botanist Alexander von Humboldt, whose knowledge of Colombia helped Linden to collect in that area. For ten years Linden persisted in his quest for orchids, rivaled only by the famous orchid collector Frederick Sander.

At the turn of the century orchidomania still held sway but showed signs of abating. English and Belgian firms dominated and the prices for unusual species were still high. In Berlin, Germany, the Otto Beyrodt firm vied with England and Brussels as a giant orchid industry. France too already had good collections. The outbreak of war in 1914 changed everything.

## The Orchid Observed

The tremendous appeal of the orchid is neither a secret nor a mystery. Quite simply orchids are unique in the plant world and bear flowers of unparalleled variety. Some orchid flowers resemble birds in flight,

Orchids resemble insects, people, birds, bees and here simple common name of "dancing ladies" applies because the orchids dance in the slightest wind.

Do you see a dancing ballerina in the center of this *Miltonia* orchid?

others suggest insects, fanciful figures, faces, or even human genitalia. With such an assortment of possible forms and colors the orchid soon became a favorite of artists and remains so today.

There are flat open flowers such as in *Phalaenopsis*; there are complex flowers as in *Stanhopea* and *Coryanthes,* frilled-edged flowers as in *Oncidiums,* pointy-petaled flowers as in *Zygopetalums,* or a lady-slipper shape as in *Paphiopedilums* or *Cypripediums.*

The *Cycnoches* orchid is frequently called the swan neck orchid because the flowers appear as graceful as a swan's neck.

*Phalaenopsis* have at times been called moth orchids because seen from a distance they might resemble a moth, and are also called dogwood orchids because of their similarity to the tree blossoms.

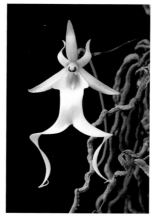

The various common names for orchids offer a clue to their immense variety. The *Anguloa* orchid from Columbia is called the tulip orchid, *Polyrrhiza* is called the frog orchid; *Phalaenopsis*, the moth orchid takes its name from the shape of the flower, as does *Coryanthes* the bucket orchid. *Miltonias* are commonly called ballerina orchids because their form suggests a ballerina and *Cycnoches* is commonly called the swan orchid because the flower resembles a swan. *Brassias*, the spider orchid bears flowers like small spiders, and the kite orchid, *Masdevallias,* also takes its name from its shape.

Another reason for the popularity of orchids with artists is that one orchid or another can always be found in bloom at any time of the year. Also, orchid flowers, with few exceptions, have amazingly long bloom times. Placed in a vial of water, many will last a week or more, a long time compared to the short vase life of roses. An artist friend of mine always complains when her rose illustrations remain unfinished because the blooms wilt in the space of just two days.

*The First Great Flower Books*
(The Illustrated Botanical Book)

The great florilegiums, which are so rare today, were volumes of plant illustrations, etched or engraved on copper before printing. These concentrated on beautiful cultivated plants rather than the medicinal plants which were illustrated in herbals. Pierre Vallett's *Le Jardin du tres Chrestien Henri IV* (1608) was perhaps the first great florilegium. The other famous florilegium was Besler's *Hortus Eyestettensis* of 1613. These volumes contained little text beyond plant names and are

The great orchid books brought forth many fancy decorative title pages. This one is from K. L. Blume's *Nova Javae*.

Harriet Miner's *Orchids: The Royal Family of Plants* is still a sought-after volume. Decorated covers like this were commonplace in fine orchid books.

beyond the scope of this book, but they lead us to the much later books on orchids.

In England more illustrated flower books were printed in the first half of the nineteenth century than in the whole of the eighteenth century, since by that time color reproduction had greatly improved. P. J. Redouté's volumes, *Choix des Belles Fleurs* and *Les Roses*, started an avalanche of florilegiums, and by the 1830s and 1840s orchid books began to proliferate.

The processes of stipple engraving, mezzotint, and aquatint were ideally suited to color work, with stipple engraving apparently the best for flower work. Sometimes several processes were used in florilegiums and this resulted in a magnificent sharpness and color especially when depicting orchids. Such volumes stunned the eye and won increasing numbers of orchid enthusiasts.

Although much praise was given to Redouté's work (and even he occasionally painted orchids) the orchid became the favorite flower to depict. It may be that few artists thought they could improve on Redouté's roses and thus most turned to orchids. At Kew, John Lindley, a devotee of orchids, published his work *Sertum Orchidaceae* (1837–38), which contains exquisite orchid portraits. Lucien Linden, another great orchid aficionado produced magnificent plates by A. Goosens for his *Iconographie des Orchidées* (1855). K. L. Blume published *Flora Javae* with most illustrations by A. J. Wendel and others. Camus' *Iconographie des Orchidées d'Europe* of 1921 illustrated the orchids of the Mediterranean basin. Finally in 1918 Henry Bolus illustrated orchids in *Orchids of the Cape Peninsula*.

Miss Taylor contributed many orchid drawings and other plates to Maund's *Botanist*.

Augusta Withers created many fine flower illustrations and was one of the premier floral illustrators, although was unrecognized in her time.

## Botanical Periodicals

In the fifty-three years from 1787 to 1840 thirty-five British botanical magazines made their first appearance. Still published today under the aegis of Kew Gardens *Curtis's Botanical Magazine* was founded by William Curtis in 1787. It appeared monthly in wrappers (paper covers) with three full-colored illustrations. At first the illustrations depicted the usual garden flowers, such as echinacea or lilies but before long readers demanded information on exotic plants including orchids. The hand-colored illustrations were striking and the principal artist from the start was Sydenham Teast Edwards (1768–1819) who joined James Sowerby, already in Curtis's employ. Both artists had a remarkable ability to capture the essence of a plant through its details.

The drawings were engraved on copper plates printed in black ink and then hand colored by several people (often women) who received little recognition for decades. Francis Sansom was the early engraver. James Sowerby's family too—women and children—

executed some of the magazine's color work. Hand-coloring at *The Botanical Magazine* continued until 1948 when it finally converted to conventional printing methods. During its long run the magazine featured such artists as Augusta Withers and S. A. Drake as well as Mary Harrison, Mrs. Taylor, and Matilda Smith and others.

From 1834 to 1878 Walter Hood Fitch was the magazine's principal artist. This master contributed perhaps the finest illustrations in the magazine's history, and today his works fetch high prices at auctions.

Ray Desmond's fine work *A Celebration of Flowers* (The Royal Botanic Gardens Kew, 1987) chronicles the first 200 years of *Curtis's Botanical Magazine*. With the clamor for information on flowers and the success of *Curtis's Botanical Magazine* competitors soon appeared. In 1815 Sydenham Edwards launched *The Botanical Register* which consisted of colored figures of exotic plants. *The Botanical Register* employed colorists and artists ranging from Sydenham Edwards himself to E. D. Smith, J. T. Hart, and other notables. Sir Joseph Paxton published sixteen volumes of the *Magazine of Botany* (1834–49) with plates drawn by F. W. Smith and lithography by Samuel Holden (Holden also produced some original drawings). However, *The Botanical Register* offered the fiercest competition to the venerable *Botanic Magazine* because its illustrations were of such fine quality.

Nurseryman and collector Conrad Loddiges, published *The Botanical Cabinet* between 1817 and 1833.

This periodical featured colored delineations from all countries. Illustrators included members of Loddiges own family and several members of the Cooke family. These publications once again depended upon fine renderings of plants, some in full color, some in half-colored versions with black-and-white details.

Benjamin Maund, an ardent plantsman, printer and bookseller, issued *The Botanist* (five volumes) in 1836. This publication published in both large and small format contained some of the most accomplished illustrations of exotics including orchids. A plethora of women artists contributed including the sisters Miss E. Maund and Miss S. Maund, Miss Nicholson, Miss Mintern, Miss Taylor, as well as Edward Dalton Smith and others. The illustrations in *The Botanist* are of the utmost beauty. The Maund sisters, along with John Stevens Henslow started *The Botanic Garden* (1825–51) which ran to thirteen volumes. Its artists included Mrs. Bury and again the Maund sisters.

Other floral publications included Lucien Linden's *Les Orchidées*, *The Floral Magazine*, *The Floral World*, among others. All contained hand-colored figures of exotic plants with an emphasis on garden flowers as well. In 1831 *The Gardener's Magazine* offered this suggestion to readers:

> ...To all the mechanical trades drawing is perhaps of more use than either writing or arithmetic. It is of immense use to a gardener, and we hope the young readers will not neglect its acquirement. He may do it by copying the cuts in this magazine.

*Gallery of Orchids
and Biographical Sketches
of the Artists*

# ACANTHOPHIPPIUM JAVANICUM

K. L. Blume, *Flora Javae*

Artist: A. J. Wendel

This is an Asiatic orchid seldom seen today. It is a terrestrial, at one time classed as an epidendrum. Found by Karl Lodewijk Blume in Java, it is an unusual orchid bearing three- to four-inch flowers every spring without much care. It was featured in the *Botanical Register* and *The Botanic Magazine* and made its introduction in the early nineteenth century. Conrad Loddiges introduced it into cultivation in 1844.

Hardly seen today it should be grown more because of its dependability and easy culture. A stunner when it first appeared in England it is not now thought of as an orchid that collectors seek.

*A. J. Wendel 1826–1915*

*Wendel was a botanical painter who lived in Leiden. He made drawings for scientific papers and from 1869 on produced drawings for various periodicals. Several of the orchid illustrations in K. L. Blume's* Nova Javae *are signed by A. J. Wendel who appears as an artist, but only occasionally in other florilegiums.*

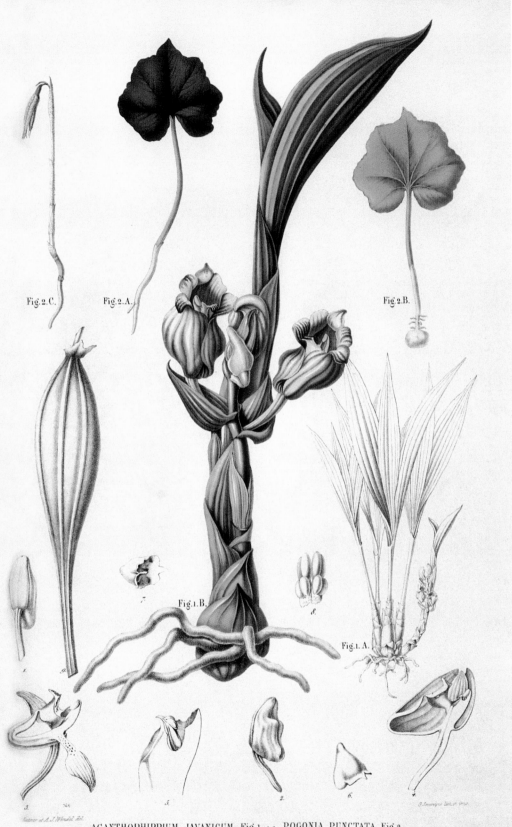

Fig.2.C.    Fig.2.A.                    Fig.2.B.

Fig.1.B.

Fig.1.A.

ACANTHOPHIPPIUM JAVANICUM. Fig.1. _ POGONIA PUNCTATA. Fig.2.

Orchid 49

# ANGRAECUM (LEONIS) VIRENS

Frederick Sander, *Reichenbachia*

Artist: H. G. Moon

A very rare plant in its day *A. leonis virens* is described in The *Botanical Magazine* in 1854 as a plant at Kew Gardens. It is indigenous to Madagascar and the island of Mauritius. Angraecums also inhabit West Africa. The variety *virens*, now obsolete, may be a form described by Hooker and Paxton as well as Dr. Lindley. It appeared in Loddiges' nursery in 1847 and later at Kew. It was first described by H. G. Reichenbach in 1885. The generic name is Latinized from *angrek*, the Malay name for all orchids of the Vanda habit of growth. Its most notable characteristic is the long tail-like spur at the base of the labellum.

The plant blooms in winter making it desirable when not much is in bloom and needs somewhat cool conditions (58F) with little light making it a fine houseplant. The flowers are star-shaped with elongated tails; some natives at the time, seeing them perched in trees thought they were insects. Some Angraecums are pollinated by small bats.

A true species, *A. leonis* grows large but today cultivated hybrids are available under different names such as *A. kotschyi* and others.

*Henry George Moon 1857–1905*

*The man who is perhaps best known for his orchid studies was at no time a pure orchid devotee but did have marital ties to the family of Frederick Sander, the Orchid King, of St. Albans, England. Moon attended art school and won prizes for his work, which includes the four-volume Reichenbachia.*

*Moon always wanted to be a barrister but his love for art won out and in 1880 he joined the art department of The Garden, a popular periodical. His work for Robinson's Flora and Sylva (1903) shows a real professional at work, for his flowers jump from the pages of that three-volume set. In 1884 Moon went to St. Albans to work for Robinson and in 1885 Frederick Sander asked him to do the drawings for the Reichenbachia book. Henry Moon was unique in that he painted with the soul of a plantsman of art and for four years he labored on Reichenbachia. He supervised the printing of this magnificent work himself. The laurels awarded to Moon for his work brought him great acclaim and recognition as the perfect botanical artist.*

*Moon married Frederick Sander's only daughter. He spent over twenty years of his life painting orchids and arguing with Sander for true-to-life paintings and against the decorative renderings that Sander wanted. Moon stuck to his guns and produced a magnificent set of plates. It is fortunate he did because it leaves behind a true picture of orchids. My plates were purchased many years ago when I started writing about orchids.*

# BATEMANIA COLLEYI

Jean Jules Linden, *Lindenia: Iconographie des Orchidées*
Artist: A. Goosens

At one time classified in the genus Zygopetalum, this fine orchid was reclassified into its own genus by James Bateman for whom is was named. It is said to have been discovered by one of Bateman's collectors in Guyana in 1834. To this day there are only a few species in this enigmatic genus. The genus was founded by Dr. Lindley as a compliment to James Bateman, a collector and enthusiast. It is named for Colley, one of Bateman's plant hunters. The plant bears lovely three-inch flowers of a brown-violet coloring and the lip is white with a reddish stain at the base. It was described in the *Botanical Register* magazine and also in Warner's *The Orchid Album*. Bateman's *Orchidaceae of Mexico and Guatemala* is a classic work of orchids.

I have only ever seen one example of this elusive orchid that resembled the Lindenia portrait, and I had grown it under the name Bollea, an entirely different genus. At the moment I make no claim for the correct name, relying on the records of the nineteenth century.

*Alfred Goosens fl. 1890*

*Goosens was the chief artist for several of Lucien Linden's publications and is cited for Linden's* Lindenia: Iconographie des Orchidées. *He was the principal artist along with Linden. Both were perfectionists and thus the orchid drawings created are supreme in detail. Although seldom cited in books, Goosens was the principal Belgian botanical artist of the times and much sought after. Most of his watercolors were engraved by G. Severeyns, a prominent and very capable engraver, and thus the result is some startlingly good orchid illustrations.*

*Goosens later collaborated with the Belgian A. C. Cogniaux on the* Dictionnaire Iconographique des Orchidées. *For both publications Goosens furnished the watercolors and both works were made using chromolithography.*

BATEMANNIA COLLEYI LINDL.

A. Goossens pinx.

J. Goffart chrom.

# BRASSAVOLA GLAUCA

James Bateman, *Orchids of Mexico and Guatemala*

Artist: Miss Drake

The Brassavolas are found in Brazil, the West Indies, and Mexico. Described by John Lindley in 1838 in *The Botanical Register*, Brassavola with its wax-like flowers appeared in 1840 and was cited in dozens of garden periodicals and seemingly had a confusing heritage being called *Bletia glauca, Laelia glauca* … and was finally classed as *B. glauca* by Dr. Lindley. H. H. Henchman is said to be the discoverer in 1837 but T. H. Hartweg also found the plant in Mexican locales. Regardless of who found it, hundreds were dumped into the market in England creating a glut, and plants were sold for ridiculously low prices.

*Miss Sarah Drake fl. 1830s–1840s*

*Since I wrote about Miss S. A. Drake in my book* Women of Flowers *(1996) other material has come forth on this woman's history (see* John Lindley, *edited by William Stearn). Her work was mainly associated with John Lindley, and with the orchids in James Bateman's* Orchidaceae of Mexico and Guatemala. *Her orchid portraits are of exquisite quality. From 1831 to 1837 Miss Drake illustrated* The Botanical Register *for Lindley. She also produced some fine work for* Transactions of the Horticultural Society *but after 1847 little work by her is recorded and she disappeared from sight.*

Pl. 16

Miss Drake del.t        M. Gauci lith.

## BRASAVOLA GLAUCA.

Pub.d by J. Ridgway & Sons, 169, Piccadilly, Dec.r 1838.

Printed by C. Hullmandel Aug.t 1st, 1842.

# CALANTHE VESTITA

Joseph Paxton, *Magazine of Botany*

Artist: S. Holden

This fine orchid from China and India deserves special mention because of its rather simple yet pretty flowers. The genus Calanthe was introduced into cultivation about 1821. Some are evergreen with leaves all year, while others are deciduous and bloom without foliage. From India and Moulein *C. vestita* was introduced by Nathaniel Wallich in 1826. *C. vestita* has dozens of forms but most carry simple flowers on a graceful stem and are white with the center marked in red. I have also grown a pure pink type. *C. vestita* is deciduous and generally blooms in winter adding to its desirability. The genus is named from the Greek, *kalos* meaning "beautiful" and *anthe* meaning "bloom". Calanthes grow from tubers and are terrestrial. Grow it with a rest when leaves fall off; water plentifully at other times.

Why is it joined here with ruellia, a garden flower? I have no idea other than to create a pleasing picture.

*Samuel Holden 1831–50*

*Samuel Holden was an ardent orchid enthusiast and an artist of some repute. His favorite flower was the orchid and he depicted the flowers beautifully in Paxton's* Magazine of Botany *(1836–49). He was working at the same time as Frederick W. Smith and exhibited at the Royal Academy.*

*The intricate flower structure of orchids and their great diversity from miniatures to large flowers attracted Holden to the plant family, as is evidenced in the fine illustrations he rendered.*

S.Holden, del & lith.

1. *Calanthe vestita*.
2. *Ruellia Purdieana*

# CATASETUM BUNGEROTHI

Jean Jules Linden, *Lindenia: Iconographie des Orchidées*

Artist: A. Goosens

This is a genus of remarkable orchids with pendulous spikes of large (up to four inches) flowers of unusual shape exhibiting a large lip. About fifty species are known from tropical America, Mexico, and Ecuador, and the flowers are more bizarre than pretty. This was a Belgian discovery and was recorded in several periodicals from 1886 onwards. The pure whiteness of the flower makes it a distinct species in this group. Many forms are available.

Unlike the flamboyant cattleya and other pretty types of orchid *C. bungerothi* did not cause very much interest when introduced in England and is practically extinct today. I have never seen a representative plant although *C. pileatum* with its yellow flowers has the same shape and form.

The name of the genus comes from the Greek *kata* meaning "down" and *seta* meaning "bristle".

CATASETUM BUNGEROTHI N. E. Brown

E. Bungeroth ad nat. del.
P. De Pannemaeker chromolithog.

# CATASETUM (STENORHYNCUS)

*Curtis's Botanical Magazine*

Artist: Lady Harriet Anne Hooker Thistleton Dyer

This is one of the few illustrations Lady Dyer created for *The Botanical Magazine*. The genus is a confusing one with some forty species from Mexico. They produce incredible flowers more bizarre than pretty and there are numerous varieties, one looking unlike another but most with a hooded petal alliance. Colors vary considerably and I have grown several of the genus. *C. scurra* had small whitish flowers, *C. pileatum* large yellow flowers, and *C. bungerothi* large white flowers. The genus even today is confusing but artists love painting the incredible structure of this orchid.

*Lady Harriet Anne Hooker Thisleton Dyer 1854–1945*

*Harriet Dyer was the eldest daughter of Sir Joseph Dalton Hooker and granddaughter of Sir William Jackson Hooker who was Director of Kew Gardens. Harriet Anne was a natural gardener and her talents were encouraged by her family. When Fitch resigned from* Curtis's Botanical Magazine *Hooker encouraged his daughter to become an illustrator, and between 1879 and 1880 Harriet Anne produced ninety drawings for the magazine. She married a man who shared her love of flowers, Sir William Turner Thistleton Dyer, a professor of natural history. From 1885 to 1905 he served as Director at Kew and his wife participated actively in welcoming the public to the Gardens. It is also said that she produced work for Charles McIntosh's books.*

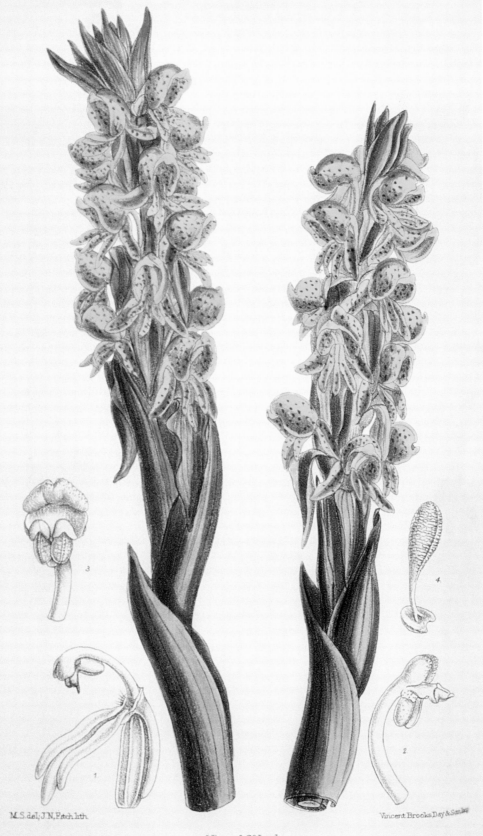

M.S.del; J.N.Fitch.lth.

Vincent Brooks Day & Son Imp

L.Reeve & C°.London

# CYCNOCHES MACULATA

Westcott & Knowles, *The Floral Cabinet*

Artist: R. Mills

This species was discovered in 1841 by William Lobb. It was described by John Lindley in *The Botanical Register* in 1843. The genus as a whole has always been confusing even to this date and were little grown in the period of orchidomania. Although signed *C. maculata* this is probably today's *C. pentadactylon*. The genus has dimorphic (male and female) flowers, which confused the early botanists. The flower shape however follows the common name of Swans' Neck Flower. Male and female flowers are distinctive in the form of the lip.

*R. Mills fl. 1830s and 1840s*

*Mills is best known for his work for Westcott and Knowles's* Floral Cabinet *(3 vols. 1837–1840). He also worked on Comte Odart's* Ampélographie Universelle *(1859). Mills's work was detailed and finely executed. He did very little other work as far as records show.*

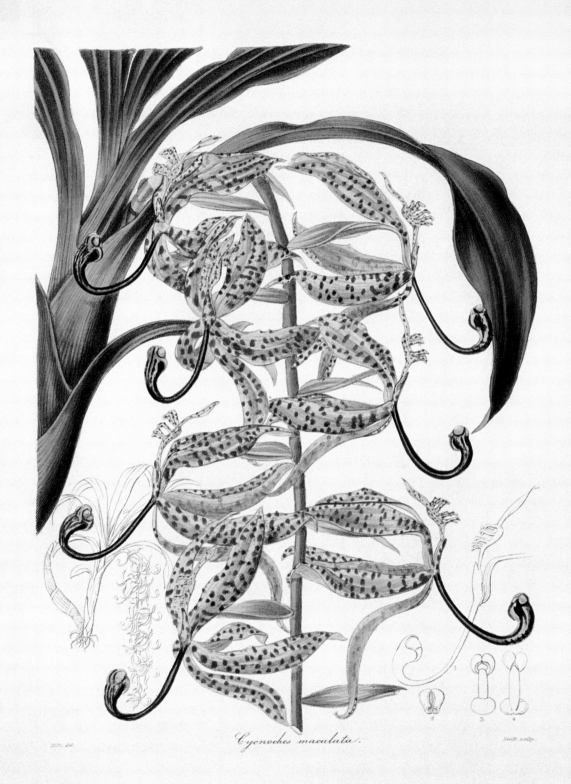

*Cycnoches maculata.*

# CYCNOCHES VENTRICOSUM

Benjamin Maund, *The Botanist*

Artist: Miss Jane Taylor

L ike the other Cycnoches in this book this species is similar in habit and has the same appearance as the rest of the genus, known as the swan orchid. It was discovered in Guatemala by George Skinner around 1830. I have never grown this species nor seen it in cultivation. As a group, the Cycnoches have gone out of favor with collectors. They are not good candidates for hybridization, being more bizarre than beautiful. It appears in Bateman's *Orchidaceae of Mexico and Guatemala*.

*Miss Jane Taylor fl. 1870s*

*I wrote about Miss Taylor in my* Women of Flowers; *she was a better artist than most people in her time gave credit for. She had a flair for orchids and was an amateur gardener herself using her knowledge of flower structure. She also painted some fine landscapes, and although there is no record of her having been schooled in art she seems to have had a natural talent. She contributed to the Society of British Artists in London and is still quite unknown in the botanical art field, but Maund at one time employed her on* The Botanist.

*Cycnoches ventricosa.*

Miss Taylor del.

# CATTLEYA GUTTATA LEOPOLDI

Emile de Puydt, *Les Orchidées*

Artist: M. Leroy

This is a distinct cattleya, its charm being the striking conglomeration of colors in both petals and lip. The original species *C. guttata* came from Rio de Janeiro in about 1827 and the variety *leopoldi* inhabits Brazil. It was introduced to cultivation in about 1850. The variety *C. amethystoglossum* which it is sometimes confused with was *C. leopoldi*.

The plant is stately in growth and unlike most large cattleya flowers rather small (about four inches across) with brilliant color combinations. It has limited use as a cocktail orchid only and was considered a novelty rather than a garden subject. Many varieties are now extinct. *C. guttata leopoldi* is seldom seen in today's collections but I did have a fine specimen of the plant for years where it bloomed faithfully every autumn with bowers of flowers.

*M. Leroy fl. 1880s*

*Monsieur Leroy was responsible for the beautiful orchid illustration in Puydt's* Les Orchidées. *The plates were produced by chromolithography and evidently retouched (redrawn and colored) by Leroy. The fifty plates in the book are the only example of the artist's work. Leroy must have been a competent artist because the orchid illustrations are amazingly good and deserve exposure. It is said he made the drawings from nature, believed to be from the collection in the greenhouses of M. Guibart. Leroy was a well-known artist of the 1880s and himself a collector of plants.*

PL. IX.___CATTLEYA GUTTATA LÉOPOLDI. ½G.

# CATTLEYA INTERMEDIA

Benjamin Maund, *The Botanist*

Artist: Mrs. Withers

This orchid was introduced from Rio de Janeiro and was sent to the Botanic Gardens at Glasgow where it flowered for the first time in 1826. A few years later it appeared at the Horticultural Society of London where it flowered in 1834.

The cattleyas constitute the most popular and important group of orchids we know because most species bear impressive flowers of pale colors that appeal to the artist's palette. Their popularity is more so today since so many hybrids have been developed, each more stunning than the next, so that cattleyas can fill a lifetime's collection. The cattleyas appear in many countries, with perhaps Brazil having the most impressive amount, but they also appear in Mexico and Guatemala.

The name *intermedia* was given to this species because of its medium size of flower compared to other cattleyas. It is a first-rate flower used for cutting and makes a fine houseplant.

*Mrs Augusta Innes Baker Withers 1792–1877*

*Mrs Withers was the daughter of a minister and did not marry till she was over thirty. Her husband was Theodore Gibson Withers, twenty years her senior. They lived in the most influential area of London in Grove Terrace, and Theodore's prominent friends encouraged Augusta both to take up and teach floral art. Her reputation earned her the position of Flower Painter in Ordinary to Queen Adelaide. During the 1830s and 1840s she produced drawings for various books and periodicals. Her illustrations for* The Botanist *are well known and she also worked for* Curtis's Botanical Magazine. *Perhaps her crowning moment was the art she rendered for James Bateman's* Orchidacea of Mexico and Guatemala *(1837–1841). She was left almost penniless when her husband died in 1869 and she herself died in 1877.*

*Cattleya intermedia.*

# CATTLEYA MOSSIAE

Harriet Miner, *Orchids: The Royal Family of Plants*
Artist: Harriet Miner

This is a native of South America and got its name in honor of Thomas Moss, an early plantsman in Liverpool, England. It was first introduced by George Green of Liverpool in 1830. In B.S. Williams' *Orchid Growers Manual* some thirty-four different varieties are listed. By whatever name the plant is majestic, with seven-inch flowers making it the largest of the labiata group. The flowers are lavender and lilac, with lip blotched red and yellow—a very attractive flower that caused much interest when first introduced in England. This orchid is most indicative of the type we know—the corsage flower—and exhibits great beauty in its large petals. It flowers in summer and generally likes a bright location and even moisture at the roots. It can grow up to thirty-six inches. The plant is still favored today and is included as a parent in many cattleya-laelia crosses (LC hybrids). Mrs. Moss of Liverpool is the namesake established in 1856. White forms are not uncommon.

*Harriet Miner 1799–1871*

*Harriet Miner was not only an artist but also dabbled in poetry and her book* Orchids: The Royal Family of Plants *(1898) is filled with sentimental poetry. Published in Boston in 1884, it was the first U.S. color plate book specifically about orchids. This accounts for its popularity and its status as a rare volume. Miner painted all the plants from live specimens so she must have had access to orchid collections or have been an orchid hobbyist herself. The orchids illustrated are not indigenous to the United States but derive rather from several tropical countries. The chromolithographic plates made on stone have the typical "wash" background which, in some instances, outstrips the color of the flowers themselves. One can safely say that Harriet Miner was a better prose writer than an artist and her writings are well worth reading.*

PLATE VII. CATTLEYA MOSSIÆ.

# CYPRIPEDIUM CAUDATUM

Emil de Puydt, *Les Orchidées*

Artist: M. Leroy

Now classified as phragmipedium, *C. caudatum* when first discovered created a sensation in Europe because of its elongated ribbon-like appendages (petals), which can reach twenty inches. It was featured in many periodicals of the times: Warner's *The Orchid Album*, *The Garden*, *Flore des Serres*, and Paxton's *Magazine of Botany*. It also at one time was called selenipedium but by any name it is a most unusual orchid, more bizarre than beautiful. Generally attributed to Peru, the plant blooms in spring and creates quite a display.

*C. caudatum (Phragmipedium)* is a stemless evergreen and the flowers are borne from the center of the plant. There are several varieties available depending upon which periodical you see; this illustration is taken from de Puydt's book. Other than as a novelty plant it cannot be classed with cattleyas or laelias for beauty.

PL. X ___ CYPRIPEDIUM CAUDATUM. (½ C.)

# CYPRIPEDIUM JAVONICA

K. L. Blume, *Flora Javae*

Artist: A. J. Wendel

Today most of the cypripediums are known as paphiopedilums, but either name denotes a slipper-type orchid. This handsome species is found in East Java and Borneo and was found by a Dutch botanist in 1823. It was named by K. L. Blume but remained unknown until John Lindley and Joseph Paxton included it in their *Flower Garden* publication. Thomas Lobb introduced the orchid into Europe in 1840. The species is beautifully drawn by either Blume himself or by A. J. Wendel, the signature on the plate.

Today most paphiopedilums are hybrids and remain similar to the common name of the lady-slipper orchid.

CYPRIPEDIUM JAVANICUM

Orchid. 58.

# CYPRIPEDIUM SEDENI

Emile de Puydt, *Les Orchidées*

Artist: M. Leroy

This orchid is said to be a cross between *C. schlimi* and *C. longifolium* and is further confused by sometimes being called paphiopedilum. By any name it is a typical lady-slipper orchid with erect stems that bear single three-inch fine red flowers. It has evergreen leaves and the flower spike arises from the center of the rosette. It is quite handsome and is an ideal subject for an artist with its regal appearance. It was a favorite plant in J. Veitch's nursery catalogue of the mid-nineteenth century. As a single decorative item *C. sendeni* makes a fine statement and is frequently used by interior designers. It was also featured in both Jennings' *Orchids,* and *The Floral Magazine,* and other publications around the year 1880. Many varieties are now available from cloning. Originally found in Colombia, Reichenbach and Lindley also had a hand it its origins.

PL. XIII.— CYPRIPEDIUM  SEDENI, (Hybride) (²⁄₃ G.)

# CYPRIPEDIUM SELLIGERUM

Jean Jules Linden, *Lindenia: Iconographie des Orchidées*

Artists: A. Goosens / P. de Pannemaeker

The cypripedium genus is huge and the hybrids created from the many species constitute hundreds of varieties each with a slight difference from the next. Sometimes called lady-slipper orchids because of the structure of the flower, many have now been classified as paphiopedilums. In any case they differ from the usual orchid flower as we know it. They are a more primitive race of orchids than any other existing form.

Recorded in *The Orchid Album* in the mid-nineteenth century this is a highly colored and diverse flower exhibiting the usual slipper-type flower in a mixture of exotic colors, mainly dull red with darker red-lined petals and a brownish lip. Crimson–purple is perhaps the dominant color.

Unlike other orchids the cypripediums have a waxy sheen to the flower that is borne from the center of a rosette of handsome green leaves. This is a terrestrial orchid preferring soil and grows in a bright place with even moisture.

CYPRIPEDIUM SELLIGERUM MAJUS

# CYRTOPODIUM PUNCTATUM

John Lindley, *Sertum Orchidaceae*

Artist: Miss Drake

The generic name of cyrtopodium is derived from *kuproc* meaning "curved" and *podion* meaning a "foot" in reference to the curved appendage of the column. *C. punctatum* is found in the West Indies and tropical America. It was described by Carl von Linné in 1759 as an epidendrum; in 1833 Lindley transferred it to cyrtopodium. It was cited in many publications of the time starting about 1880 and ironically is better known today than it was in its time. It is a large plant, unusual for an orchid, tall and terrestrial. At one time it went under the name *Epidendrum punctatum*. Little is written about this orchid in nineteenth-century orchid manuals, and yet it is a noble plant.

Pl. 12.

*Cyrtopodium punctatum.*

Miss Drake, del.	M. Gauci, lith.

Publd. by J. Ridgway & Sons, 169 Piccadilly, July 1, 1838.

Printed by P. Gauci.

# CYRTOPODIUM WILLMOREI (ANDERSONI)

Westcott & Knowles, *The Floral Cabinet*

Artist: R. Mills

This handsome flower is often confused with *C. punctatum* in today's trade. It is found in Mexico and Florida (where I have seen it) and it is said that Carl von Linné introduced the genus in 1759 as an epidendrum. John Lindley transferred it to cyrtopodium in 1833 although Robert Brown, it is claimed, made the change in 1813. In any case it was discovered by Dr. J. Anderson and bears his name. These are large plants growing up to sixty inches and there are only a few species known. It is terrestrial and in warm climates can be grown in the garden.

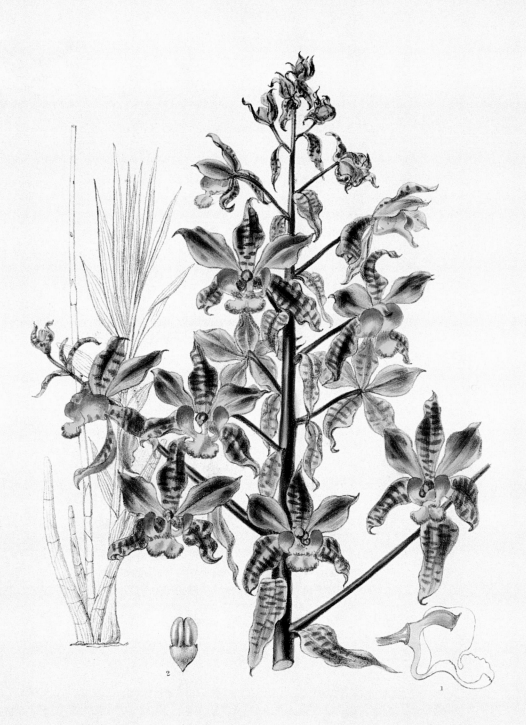

R. Mills del.                                               Printed by J. Graf.

*Cyrtopodium Willmorei.*

# DENDROBIUM FARMERI

Edward Step, *Favourite Flowers of Garden and Greenhouse*
Artist: B. Herincq

This dendrobium was introduced from India in 1847 and then again in 1864 from Moulmein, sent by Dr. McClelland from the Calcutta Botanic Garden to Mr. W. G. Farmer of Nonesuch Park in Surrey. It bears the latter's name. It was also bloomed by Baron Schroeder in Staines.

The chrome-yellow flowers make it an ideal choice for the artists' brush and the plant's pendulous flower stalk adds to its grace. Because the dendrobes are such a large family *D. farmeri* is seldom seen in collections, and is outranked by the new hybrid dendrobiums that offer a choice of color from white to pink. It is, however, an historical plant having been in cultivation for many years and thus worthy of mention.

*D. farmeri* needs a three-month rest during the year with little water. It generally blooms in spring. Because of its pendulous habit and profusion of flowers artists filled books with portraits of the plant—at least a dozen publications cited the plant.

*B. Herincq 1820–91*

*A botanist and plant collector Madame B. Herincq was born in Villejuif near Paris. She was a collaborator on a horticultural manual by Jacques. The fine illustrations in Step's* Favourite Flowers of Garden and Greenhouse *are attributed to Madame Herincq, but were taken from George D. Bois's* Atlas des Plantes de Jardin. *Bois was Assistant to the Professor of Culture at the Natural History Museum in Paris. Madame Herincq also worked for other botanical volumes of the time and was considered a talented artist.*

B. HERINCQ

**DENDROBIUM FARMERI,** *var. aureoflavum*

Nat. size

PL. 238

# DENDROBIUM HEDYOSMUM   (D. scabrilingue)

*Curtis's Botanical Magazine*

Artist: W. H. Fitch

This species is designated as *D. hedyosmum* but in its time was known as *D. scabrilingue*. It was discovered by Thomas Lobb in 1849 in Moulmein and described to John Lindley in the Journal of the Linnean Society. In 1862 it was sent to Low & Company under yet another name but James Bentham changed the name to *D. hedyosmum* (sweet-scented) in reference to its lovely fragrance. It is a handsome species with its typical pendent flower scape and fine flowers, but extinct today as far as we know.

*Walter Hood Fitch 1817–92*

*So much has been written and said about W. H. Fitch as a talented botanical artist that it is difficult to add any new noteworthy information. This man contributed some 10,000 drawings to various publications. He was originally a calico printer and came to Joseph Hooker who employed him as a full-time artist for* The Botanical Magazine. *His first plate appeared in 1814 when he was just seventeen and, incredibly, he produced illustrations for the magazine for forty years. He lithographed his own drawings. He continually argued with Hooker about monies and eventually left the magazine. He was granted a civil list pension which continued until his death in 1892.*

W. Fitch, del et lith.

Vincent Brooks, Imp.

# DENDROBIUM MACROPHYLLUM

Emile de Puydt, *Les Orchidées*

Artist: M. Leroy

This orchid is a remarkable plant that bears pale lilac flowers on leafless stems but sometimes retains its foliage. The stems are pendulous reaching two feet and are crowded with three-inch flowers, as many as one hundred to a plant. When introduced into cultivation (first recorded in 1845 in *Gardener's Chronicle*) it caused quite a stir in England. *D. macrophyllum* (sometimes called *superbum*) comes from the Philippines and is still grown today. I had a magnificent specimen that must have weighed twenty pounds and each spring rewarded me with about two hundred sweet-smelling (rhubarb-scented) flowers.

You have to grow *D. superbum* in baskets and treat it with kind neglect. It resents much pampering and once during the year it must be kept quite dry for two months. Varieties of this species have been used for room decorations to beautiful effect.

PL. XVII. _ DENDROBIUM MACROPHYLLUM (½ G)

# DENDROBIUM NOBILE  (Comparetia coccinea)

Benjamin Maund, *The Botanist*

Artist: Miss Taylor

This lovely orchid was named *Comparetia* in its early cultivation. A miniature orchid with brilliant red broad lip, today it is properly known as a *Dendrobium nobile* or wardainum group. The illustration comes from Maund's *The Botanist*, a periodical published between 1842 and 1846 and shows the fine talent of Miss Taylor who painted many orchid portraits but was hardly recognized in her time.

*D. nobile* was collected in China by John Reeves and first described by John Lindley in 1830. There are many varieties of this species and it is widely grown today.

*Comparettia coccinea*

# DENDROBIUM NOBILE    (type)

Edward Step, *Favourite Flowers of Garden and Greenhouse*

Artist: B. Herincq

This dendrobium is one of the most commonly
cultivated of the genus and has many forms of
color variation running from pink to almost cerise.
Originally it was collected by John Reeves in China
and John Lindley described it in his *General Species
of Orchidaceous Plants* of 1830. It is also found in
Thailand and Laos. *D. nobile* is frequently used as a
lei flower in Hawaii and the species is responsible
for many varieties today.

**DENDROBIUM NOBILE**

Nat. size

PL. 237

# DISA GRANDIFLORA

Henry Bolus, *Orchids of the Cape Peninsula*

Artist: H. Bolus

Known as the Pride of the Table Mountains D. *grandiflora* is found in various parts of South Africa. It is a very showy terrestrial with fantastic blue flowers. From 1875 on it was described in dozens of botanical periodicals famous for its rare blue coloring. Henry Bolus suggested that the name originated from *dis* meaning "rich". Disas were described as early as 1767 and although *uniflora* now goes under the name D. *grandiflora*, one is brilliant red while the other species is blue, so confusion reigns in this category. The blue species is described today as D. *hamatopetela*. The genus was described by several botanists and at one time even went under the name of *Satyrium grandiflora*.

*Henry Bolus 1834–1911*

*A Cape Town stockbroker and amateur botanist, Harry Bolus migrated to England in his teens. He did menial jobs for years and finally became a stockbroker. Within twenty years he made his fortune. His fascination for orchids made him a prime candidate to hunt and find orchids which he sketched with great talent, and he corresponded with Sir Joseph Dalton Hooker about local plants. In ensuing years he devoted his time to plants, finding pleasure in new specimens. In 1888 he wrote* Orchids of the Cape Peninsula. *He drew and described all the plants from nature; the plates in his book are strikingly effective both in detail and decoration. He also had an interest in ferns and contributed materials for* A List of the Flowering Plants and Ferns of the Cape Peninsula. *He was a humanitarian and contributed much money to the South African College for the future of plant research. He was a member of the Linnean Society and died of a heart seizure in 1911.*

Tab. 83

H. Bolus del

Miles Lith, London.W.

DISA GRAMINIFOLIA, *KER.*

# DISA UNIFLORA

Frederick Burbridge, *Cool Orchids*

Artist: F. Burbridge

Rare and beautiful *D. uniflora* is from South Africa's Table Mountain area, and is a showy terrestrial species. The blooms are brilliantly colored. *The Gardener's Chronicle* in 1875 named it *D. grandiflora* but it is generally called *D. uniflora* today. Because of its rare red color and dissimilarity to other orchids the plant was described in the mid-nineteenth century in numerous publications; almost every famous periodical of the times featured an illustration of Disa. In the late nineteenth century large shipments of this incredible orchid were brought to England.

This is a premier orchid and quite difficult to bloom in cultivation. It is rarely attempted by artists because it was considered more a novelty orchid rather than a commercial one, yet its flower is truly exotic. Once Disas were common in South Africa, but today they are few.

It is grown as a terrestrial and a mature plant can bear many flowers—usually in early fall. It is called the "Pride of the Table Mountain". There is also a blue variety.

*Frederick William Thomas Burbridge 1847–1905*

*Frederick Burbridge was a prolific orchid artist and probably most famous for his 1875 book* The Narcissus. *When young he was a gardener at Kew and his experiences there formed the foundation for his plant knowledge. He was on the editorial staff of* The Garden *and collected plants for J. Veitch in Borneo and Sierra Leone. He was one of the artists and lithographers for Jennings'* Orchids and How to Grow Them in India *(1875). He was educated at home and was an avid orchid hunter returning thousands of species to England. He eventually received the Victoria Medal and became curator at Trinity College Botanic Garden in Dublin. He died aged 68.*

1. DISA GRANDIFLORA.
2. Pollen masses.    3. Stigmatic surface

# EPIDENDRUM CILIARE

*Curtis's Botanical Magazine*

Artist: Miss Taylor

In 1737 Linnaeus referred to all orchids as epidendrums but this did not please the experts. In due course Olof Swartz, John Lindley, and Robert Brown also went along with the classification of this orchid as an epidendrum. Epidendrums are found worldwide: South America, Central America, and the West Indies for example. This genus became quite crowded with orchids from all parts of the world, and changes are continually made even to this day as most nurseries now class some epidendrums as encyclias. The plants bloom freely with small but impressive flowers.

With so many changes in the genus it is almost impossible to guarantee this plant as *E. umbellatum* today and is no doubt renamed a different species of the genus whether epidendrum or encyclia.

In 1853 in *Folio Orchidacea* there were 300 species cited. Then in 1861 *Reichenbachia* reclassified the genus and James Bentham in his *Genera Planterum* in 1883 again classed them as epidendrums.

S. Edwards del.    Pub. by W. Curtis S.ᵗ Geo: Crescent Dec. 1. 1799.    F Sanfom sculp.

# EPIDENDRUM FRAGRANS

*Curtis's Botanical Magazine*

Artist: Sydenham Edwards

This genus is large and at one time almost any tropical orchid was thrown into the group by Linnaeus. There are species from many parts of the world: India, Africa, Mexico, and South America for example. *E. fragrans* flowered for the first time in 1778 and plants were seen in the Apothecaries Garden at Chelsea in 1796. With its fragrant, small, pretty flowers this species is still popular today.

*Sydenham Teast Edwards 1769–1819*

*This man was a consummate artist and his botanical illustrations won him great fame. He contributed some 2,000 plates to* The Botanical Magazine *and eventually started his own periodical,* The Botanical Register. *He was the son of a schoolmaster and had a fondness for plants, copying illustrations from* Flora Londinensis. *A friend of the family showed the drawings to William Curtis who thought the boy had great talent and brought him to London to train him in botanical art. He was about twenty years old when his first illustration appeared in Curtis's Botanical Magazine of 1788. In addition to his floral drawings he also addressed nature subjects such as birds. After he started his magazine* The Botanical Register *he lived only four years and died in 1819.*

Pub April 1 1791 by W Curtis S' Georges Crescent

# LAELIA AUTUMNALIS

Harriet Miner, *Orchids: The Royal Family of Plants*
Artist: Harriet Miner

Cattleyas and laelias have a close alliance to each other, and resemble each other in structure and form as well as in color. The flowers are large, glamorous, and very desirable. There are several forms but *L. autumnalis* was first mentioned in writing in 1836 when it was received from Mexico and recorded by James Bateman. John Lindley also recorded the orchid in 1831. It was imported in quantity by Loddiges Nursery in London. Several forms of *L. autumnalis* exist and *Reichenbachia* classed it as a hybrid. The plant exhibits large seven-inch flowers of pale pink to magenta coloring, many on an arching stem, in the middle of summer.

Its popularity in England was dwarfed by the cattleya genera which was the rage at the time, but today the laelias have come into their own and are much sought after by collectors. They are an elegant flower and respond well to cattleya conditions, namely bright light and even moisture. Many legends of a romantic nature abound about laelias but none have any authenticity.

PLATE IX.   LAELIA AUTUMNALIS.

# LAELIA SUPERBIENS

James Bateman, *Orchidaceae of Mexico and Guatemala*

Artist: Miss Drake

This remarkable orchid was discovered by G. Ure Skinner and the genus was named by John Lindley. The laelia itself was borrowed from the Romans who, it is said, had daughters of this name.

The plant was introduced in 1842 by the Horticultural Society of London through Theodor Hartweg. In its native Guatemala it was used as a garden flower by the Indians and was planted near the entrances of homes. It was called the Wand of St. Joseph by the Indians because of its beautiful large flowers. There are several varieties and today the plant is considered a prize find, revered for its beauty and stalwart appearance. A mature plant may have as many as fifty glamorous flowers. It was described by Dr. Lindley in *The Botanical Register* in 1840.

Pl. 38.

LÆLIA SUPERBIENS.

Mrs. Drake, del.t     M. Gauci, lith.

Pub.d by J. Ridgway & Sons, 169, Piccadilly, March, 1843.

Printed by J. Brooks.

# LAELIA, DENDROBIUM, MAXILLARIA

Charles McIntosh, *The Greenhouse*

Artist: Elizabeth Twining (attr.)

Orchids in bouquets were a rare occurrence in general and especially here where three species are detailed, yet they never bloom at the same time. Nonetheless, the bouquet is included here because the flowers are drawn with infinite beauty and are botanically correct. At the time the laelia was one of the favorite orchids and dendrobiums were also quite well known, but the maxillaria was quite rare (as it is today).

Because orchids were at the time rarely considered cut flowers, the bouquet is unusual. Further, the flowers were not considered long-lasting—another fallacy.

*Elizabeth Twining 1805–89*

*Twining was born into the famous tea family who still continues today. She displayed talent as a miniaturist and was also involved in helping the poor. While in Brussels in 1827 she started working on botanical art. She was a devotee of* Curtis's Botanical Magazine *and in 1849 she finally published her own landmark book in two volumes,* Illustrations of the Natural Order of Plants. *These drawings, based on plants at the Royal Botanic Gardens at Kew, were greeted with great acclaim.*

Lœlia Anceps.

Maxillaria Harrisoniæ.        Dendrobium Moschatum.

# MAXILLARIA TENUIFLORA  (Picta)

*Curtis's Botanical Magazine*

Artist: Miss Harrison

This orchid was originally pictured in *Curtis's Botanical Magazine* in 1832, an early entry for this genus. The name maxillaria refers to the maxilla or jaw bone, comparing the yawning flowers of column and lip, as viewed from the side, to the jaws of an insect. *M. tenuiflora (picta)* flowered in the Chiswick Gardens of the Royal Horticultural Society in 1839.

A native of Mexico, this is a rare plant seldom seen today and we only have pictures of it to prove its existence. Its orange-yellow colored petals spotted with crimson makes it a pretty plant but not overly impressive. Most maxillarias are not as showy as the more impressive orchids such as laelias and cattleyas. That was the situation in the nineteenth century and it remains the same today.

*Mary Harrison 1788–1875*

*Mary Harrison was a natural artist from a very early age, although most of her life was taken up caring for her sick mother. However, her father recognized her talent and encouraged her art. To escape her family she married young and on her honeymoon in France discovered the Louvre Museum, which gave her the inspiration to paint flowers. While painting a little over the next few years, she began in earnest only when her husband became sick and she realized she had to make a living to support the family. She joined the Society of Painters in Watercolor.*

*She favored painting horticultural and botanical subjects, becoming very proficient. When Queen Victoria purchased two of her paintings she became in demand and Curtis's Botanical Magazine employed her to do some of their work.*

*Mary Harrison continued her floral pursuits with success until she died in 1875.*

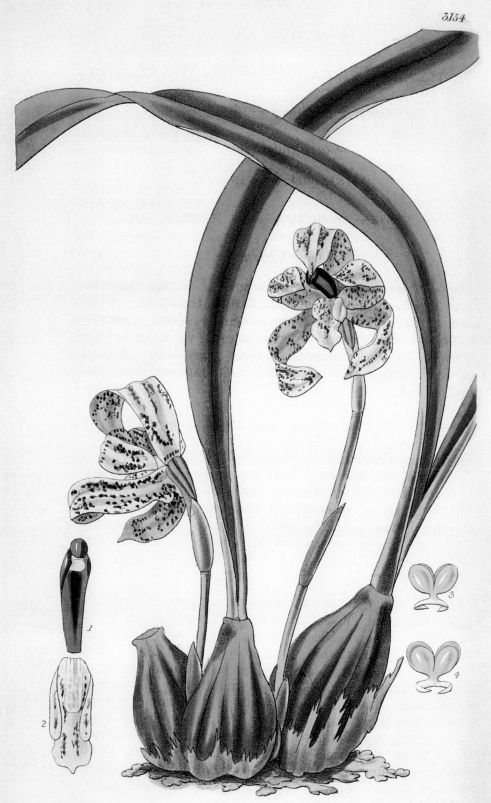

Mrs Arnold Harrison.                Pub. by S. Curtis Glazenwood Essex Mar.1.1832.                Swan Sc

# ODONTOGLOSSUM CRISPUM

Edward Step, *Favorite Flowers of Garden and Greenhouse*

Artist: B. Herincq

During the 1840s an array of odontoglossums was imported into England. The name comes from the Greek words for tooth and tongue. The plants are natives of the Andes and grow at high altitudes, about 6,000 feet. This plant, probably the most impressive in the genus because of its frilled petals and pure whiteness, has at times been called *O. alexandrea* but is more commonly known as *O. crispum*. It was collected in 1841 in the Colombian Andes by Theodor Hartweg but did not appear in cultivation until twenty years later. There are several odontoglossums still grown today but this species far outranks the others in beauty. In its heyday it was revered for its beautiful flowers and long blooming times from January to April. It was described in dozens of publications: *The Orchid Album, Floral Magazine, Lindenia,* and *Reichenbachia.* B. S. Williams in his manual of 1894 lists dozens of varieties.

O. *crispum* needs coolness (58° F) at night and requires little water but needs some bright light. It is supposedly a plant revered in religious ceremonies in Mexico where it is also found in the mountainous regions.

B. HERINCQ

ODONTOGLOSSUM CRISPUM

Nat. size

PL. 241

# ODONTOGLOSSUM LUTEO PURPUREUM

Jean Jules Linden, *Lindenia: Iconographie des Orchidées*

Artist: A. Goosens

This orchid was discovered by Jean Jules Linden in 1842 in the forests of the Cordillera Central of New Granada in South America at a high elevation, about 7,000 feet, an unusual altitude for orchids. Most collectors had thought that all came from tropical areas. It was described and named by John Lindley and came into cultivation for a short time. It then disappeared and was rediscovered by the Horticultural Society of London years later. The species has such a wide range in the mountains where other odontoglossums are found that it has at times created confusion and was renamed several times (once in 1868) by *Reichenbachia* as the xenia species.

This orchid is quite variable and colors may be rather faded and not as popular as many other odontoglossums. In some areas it was known as the tiger orchid because of the brown and yellow coloring and perhaps is our *Odontoglossum grande* that we grow today. *The Gardener's Chronicle* at one time listed three to five different forms.

ODONTOGLOSSUM LUTEO-PURPUREUM Lindl.

P. De Pannemaeker del.

# ONCIDIUM LIMMINGHEI

Jean Jules Linden, *Lindenia: Iconographie des Orchidées*

Artists: A. Goosens / P. de Pannemacher

One could not find a prettier representative of a small orchid than *O. Limminghei* that blooms in June and July. The plant boasts hundreds of flowers on long stems and generally grows on tree trunks. Like many oncidiums it comes from Mexico and other tropical areas and is easily cultivated. It was first discovered by Professor Morren of Liège and sent from Venezuela to Belgium. It first flowered in 1855 and was sent to John Lindley in time for insertion into one of his publications. The species was dedicated to Comte Alfred Limminghe who was an orchid devotee in Belgium.

The plant is very desirable because of its ease of culture, needing only warmth and some sun. It is sometimes referred to as the Dancing Lady orchid because the flowers move in the slightest wind. The genus also includes *O. macranthum, O. wentworthianum* and others with similar small flowers generally of brown and yellow color. *O. limminghei* is described in many publications and is still grown today in several varieties.

ONCIDIUM LIMMINGHEI ED. MORREN.

# ONCIDIUM SUPERBIENS

Frederick Sander, *Reichenbachia*

Artist: H.G. Moon

This is a huge genus and boasts some outstanding, generally small yellow and brown orchids, many to a plant. *O. superbiens* is native to the eastern Cordillas of New Granada at high elevations (sometimes 9,000 feet) and is probably the queen of the genus. It was first described in 1847 by Louis Schlim. This plant is quite similar to *O. macranthum* but the flower is a darker brown. A well-grown plant can have some fifty flowers on very pretty, wand-like stems.

H. G. Reichenbach first described the species and it was later included in various periodicals of the time.

*O. superbiens* is free flowering and a mature plant can bear hundreds of flowers. Hybrids of the type make a handsome interior decoration because the plant bears flowers on graceful stems which makes it a favorite with artists.

GUSTAV LEUTZSCH, CHROMOLITH. GERA, REUSS.

ONCIDIUM SUPERBIENS.

# ORCHIS PURPUREA

Edmund Gustave Camus, *Iconographie des Orchidées d'Europe*

Artist: E. G. Camus

This genus gives its name to the whole order. They are natives of Europe with small flowers, hardly glamorous, and seldom seen in cultivation today. The plants have erect flower spikes and bear hundreds of blossoms. The plants appeared in and out of culture in the early years of the eighteenth and nineteenth century but through the decades have disappeared in collections and are extremely difficult to transplant to gardens as they are temperamental about their habitat. They are similar to the North American lady slipper in their specific wants.

*Edward Gustav Camus 1852–1915*

*Camus was a botanist and pharmacist. He was an excellent illustrator very keen on detail and worked at the Natural History Museum in Paris (1908). He was the author of numerous botanical works: his* Iconographie des Orchidées d'Europe et du Bassin Méditerranean *was a mammoth enterprise and a comprehensive work on the orchids of the Mediterranean region. He was born and died in Paris.*

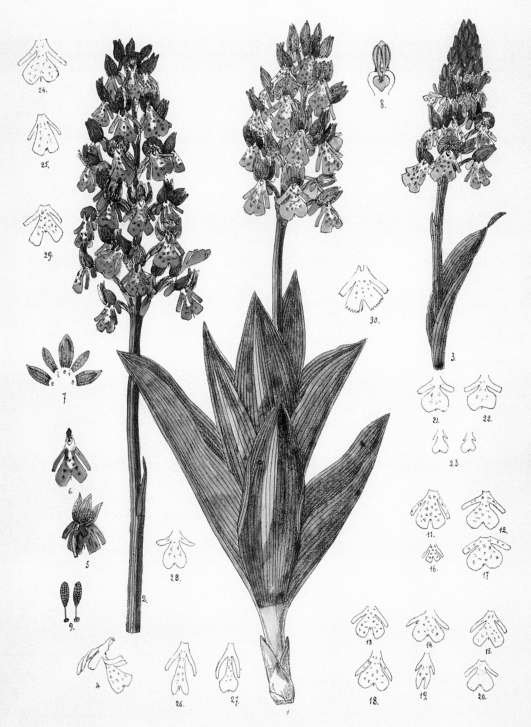

ORCHIS PURPUREA Hudson.

# PERISTERIA    (Elata)

Jean Jules Linden, *Lindenia: Iconographie des Orchidées*

Artist: A. Goosens

Called the dove orchid from the Greek word *eplorepa, P. elata* and is noted for its fine four-inch, globular, very waxy, flower which looks as though it has been carved from marble. The dove plant supposedly resembles the bird because inside the petals is a figure of a white dove. It is also sometimes called the Holy Ghost plant. From Panama, this orchid is the national flower of the country and also played a part in supernatural rituals.

It was brought into cultivation in 1826 and sent to Mr. Harrison, a plant devotee. It is a terrestrial plant and is still seen today in preferred collections. It makes a magnificent subject for the artist's brush. Colors vary considerably as seen in this illustration.

PERISTERIA ASPERSA ROLFE

A. Goossens pinx.

P. De Pannemaeker chrom.

# PHAIUS BLUMEI

K. L. Blume, *Collections des Orchidées les Plus Remarquables de L'Archipel Indien et du Japon*

Artist: A. J. Wendel

One can hardly imagine the astonishment of the British orchid world when this plant appeared in about 1890. Here was a very large, stately, erect plant with broad leaves and large highly colored flowers. Orchids were generally thought of as fanciful, delicate, and pretty; *P. blumei* was bold and noble in appearance and a terrestrial. Coming from Asia, India, Ceylon, the Philippines, Australia, and China and most notably found by Blume in Java any orchid enthusiast would marvel at *P. blumei*.

In Blume's work the plant is drawn full scale from nature. Blume, Fantin Latour, and A. J. Wendel were some of the artists and G. Severeyns was the fine engraver. It is interesting to note that phaius plants—and there are several species of the genus—are now sold as garden subjects in tropical climates and are readily available at nurseries. My stand of *P. tankervillea* (*grandifolius*) grows on its own, multiplying year after year in my Florida backyard.

PHAJUS BLUMEI.

Orchid. 1

# PHALAENOPSIS SCHILLERIANA

Robert Warner and Benjamin S. Williams, *Select Orchidaceous Plants*
Artist: James Andrews

This is a startlingly beautiful orchid that offers bowers of white flowers on arching stems. It was introduced in 1858 from Manila by Consul Schiller of Hamburg and bloomed in his conservatory for the first time in Europe in 1860: it is thus dedicated to him. In the following year a French importer sent the plant to B. S. Williams and it flowered in Robert Warner's collection in 1862 in England. The plant bears large tessellated leaves and prefers growing on tree branches with good light and excellent air circulation. It seems to have much color variation, some with white flowers while others in my collection are of a pink shade.

It is interesting to note that James Andrews created the drawing. Andrews was never considered a consummate artist by the experts of his time but as I leaf through many books on orchids James Andrews' orchid illustrations seem better than most artists for decorative effect and beauty.

*James Andrews 1801–65*

*Andrews was an artist who was rarely given credit for his talent in his time. He made scores of drawings for a variety of books including* Warner's Orchid Album. *He also figured in dozens of other botanical books as well as "language of flower" books. Andrews had a true gift for observing flowers. He was born in Walmouth and was no relation to the artist H. C. Andrews. His early life is vague but he published artwork when he was about thirty-five years old. In my library I have his* Flora's Gems *and the* Treasures of the Parterre *with verses by Louisa Anne Twamley produced in 1837, and his work had great charm and delicacy. He also made drawings for Robert Tyas' many sentimental books. In his day he was underrated and scolded by the dean of botanical art research, Wilfred Blunt, for whiling away his talents with obscure sentimental books. However, today, James Andrews' illustrations command great prices at auction.*

J.ᵈ Andrews, del. et. lith.   Phalænopsis Schilleriana.   W. West imp.

# PHALAENOPSIS STUARTIANA

Harriet Miner, *Orchids: The Royal Family of Plants*

Artist: Harriet Miner

First discovered by Boxall on the Philippine island of Mindanao in 1881 this fine orchid was named for the owner of the Low Nursery, Stuart Low. The plant produces an arching stem of white flowers with a red-and-yellow spotted lip, creating a rather handsome plant. Many flowers are carried on a stem and although small at two inches, it creates a bower of beauty. It was recorded in *The Gardener's Chronicle* as well as *The Orchid Album* and several other periodicals, as it caused great interest in the orchid world of the time.

I have grown this plant recently and it is of easy culture and the flower lasts for several weeks making it very desirable. Its beauty is revered in its native land where it is used in leis and floral decorations at festivals.

PLATE XI.

PHALENOPSIS STUARTIANA.

# RENANTHERA MUTUTINA

Jean Jules Linden, *Lindenia: Iconographie des Orchidées*

Artists: A. Goosens / P. de Pannamacher

Dating back to about 1824 and discovered by K. L. Blume this very rare species from Java is now similar to, if not, *imschootiana,* and was named by John Lindley. Some books class it as of dwarf habit but my plant grows to about three feet with dozens of speckled red and orange flowers on graceful stems. The generic name is from *ren,* "a kidney", and *anthera* "kidney-shaped" pollinia.

It is reported to have figured in the Rothschild collection in the nineteenth century. The flowers are produced in abundance and a mature plant can boast one hundred three-inch flowers. James Veitch considers this plant *R. micrantha* and cited it in the *Botanical Register* of 1843.

Fairbanks, a gardener in England in 1813 grew the plants in baskets with great results, but it is not readily grown today.

C. De Bruyne pinx.

P. De Pannemaeker et fils chrom.

RENANTHERA MATUTINA LINDL.

# SATYRIUM LUPULINUM

Henry Bolus, *Orchids of the Cape Peninsula*

Artist: Henry Bolus

These orchids are native to Northern India and South Africa, and have disappeared from cultivation. They gained the name "satyr" decades ago and are steeped in lore and mysticism:

*Among the early Romans the orchid family was often called Satyrion because it was believed to be the food of the satyrs and as such excited them to those excesses which were characteristic of the attendants of Bacchus. Hence, the orchid's root, not unnaturally, became famous as a powerful stimulant (passion) medicine and is so described by all Herbalists from the time of Dioscorides.*

Richard Folkard, *Plants, Lore, Legends and Lyrics*

Bolus made a study of this genus and discovered many species all with rather insignificant flowers. The name was used by Dioscorides and Pliny probably from the Greek mythology (the satyr is noted for lasciviousness) and the plant was considered in its time an aphrodisiac.

Tab. 28

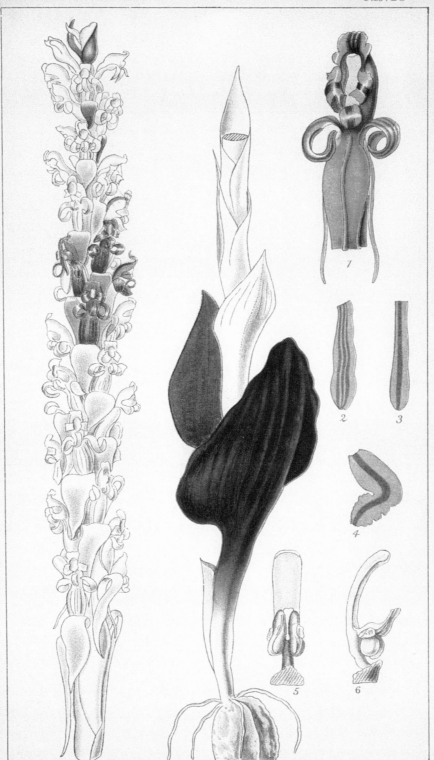

H. Bolus del. ad vivam, 13.10.1890.

Miles Lith, London.W.

SATYRIUM LUPULINUM, *LINDLEY*.

# SCHOMBURGKIA MARGINATA

John Lindley, *Sertum Orchidaceae*

Artist: Schouten

The genus Schomburgkia is named for Dr. Richard Schomburg, a German botanist on an expedition to British Guyana in 1840–44. Schomburg was director of the Botanic Gardens at Adelaide in Australia. Other species of Schomburgkia had been discovered in previous years and the species illustrated in Lindley's work may well be S. *tibicinis* which hailed from Honduras. The plant I bloomed with six-foot spikes resembled the latter species. Because of its gigantic proportions it caused a great stir among orchid enthusiasts in England and Lindley furthered its reputation.

*Schouten fl. 1830s and 1840s*

*Little is known about Schouten but his knowledge of orchids was excellent and his drawings in Lindley's* Sertum Orchidaceae *show that he certainly knew flowers. He was in the company of some very fine artists, working alongside Sarah Drake, who produced the major part of the illustrations for Lindley's book. William Griffith and Richard Schomburg also contributed to this famous volume. The illustrations were further enhanced by the engravings of M. Gauci. The orchid* Schomburgkia tibicinis *is a very difficult flower to portray and his rendering is excellent.*

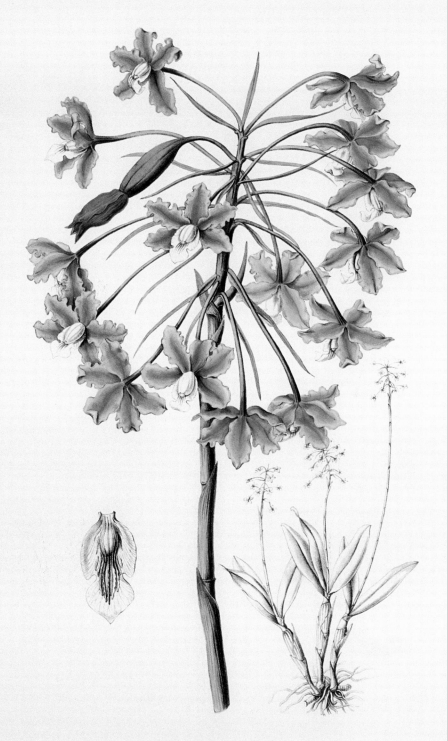

*Schomburgkia marginata.*

Schauium, del.

M. Gauci, lith.

Pub.d by J. Ridgway & Sons, 169, Piccadilly, July 1, 1838.

Printed by P. Gauci.

# SOBRALIA MACRANTHA

James Bateman, *Orchids of Mexico and Guatemala*
Artist: Miss Drake

This tall reed-like orchid is an anomaly in the Orchidaceae because the flowers only last a few days. In 1794 the genus was named for Dr. Francisco Sobral, a Spanish physician and botanist. *S. macrantha* was found by Theodor Hartweg and G. Ure Skinner in 1841 and described by John Lindley in 1836 in *Sertum Orchidaceae*. This is a regal plant growing to six or eight feet and bears large stunning red flowers lasting a day or two, one flowering after the other. My own plant stayed in bloom for some three weeks. It is a terrestrial and one of the showy orchids loved by England in its time and equally revered today (when available).

Pl. 37.

M[?]S Drake, del[?]                                                                                   M. Gauci, lith.

S O B R A L I A   M A C R A N T H A .

Pub[d] by J. Ridgway & Sons, 169, Piccadilly July 1842.

Printed by P. Gauci.

# SOPHRONITIS GRANDIFLORA

Robert Warner and Benjamin S. Williams, *The Orchid Album*
Artist: J. Nugent Fitch

This lovely miniature orchid was gathered by G. Gardner in Brazil in about 1836, but some plants were discovered years before. S. *grandiflora* is sometimes called S. *coccinea* or S. *cernu*. The name sophronitis is derived from the Greek word *sophron* meaning "modest", but is hardly appropriate for the blazing red flowers of this fine plant. Because of its spectacular display it was recorded by numerous periodicals from 1842 on—its red flowers make a stunning illustration. There are several varieties.

In recent years the sophronitis genus has been used extensively in hybridization to bring red color into other orchid flowers. The results have been excellent.

*John Nugent Fitch 1840–1927*

*Walter Hood Fitch's nephew John followed in his uncle's footsteps and became the artist for* The Botanical Magazine *in 1878. He continued for many years, producing about 2,500 plates. He had the same talent for picturing a plant in his mind and being able to portray it in a decorative manner in the same way as did his uncle. John also did numerous illustrations for Warner's* The Orchid Album *and these were considered outstanding. He was also a competent lithographer. Although he never received the recognition of his famous uncle, he deserves to be noted as one of the finest draughtsman of flowers. He stopped drawing when his hands became afflicted with arthritis.*

SOPHRONITIS GRANDIFLORA.

# STANHOPEA INSIGNIS

Conrad Loddiges and Sons, *The Botanical Cabinet*

Artist: G. Cooke

S tanhopeas have a remarkable flower structure with inverted petals and blossoms borne on hanging stems from the bottom of the plant. They are frequently called "little bulls" because of their horn-like appendages. The stanhopeas are native to tropical America with many in Mexico or of Brazilian heritage. The flowers are large and short-lived and emit a strong camphor-like scent. The plant is identified in *The Botanical Register* in 1885 and in *The Botanical Cabinet* in 1885. However the plant was introduced to Kew Gardens in 1829 and flowered there. It also flowered in William Cattley's collections the next year. *S. insignis* was originally found by Alexander von Humboldt and José Antonio Bonpland in Ecuador thus its heritage is questionable. Today it is more popularly thought of as a Brazilian plant.

At the time *The Botanical Cabinet* was printed, there were black-and-white and color renditions on the same plate as in my edition.

*George Cooke 1781–1834*

*Born in London, George Cooke was the son of a German candy maker. He became an excellent engraver and made numerous plates from 1802 mainly on topographical subjects. His attraction to flowers allowed him to create about 2,000 drawings for Conrad Loddiges' Botanical Cabinet (1817–33). Cooke drew some 850 plates and Loddiges 833 plates. At the time these were not considered of great value but gradually the true value of the flower paintings came to be recognized. Cooke worked with his brother, William, to produce* The Southern Coast of England *(1814–26) with 40 plates after J. M. W. Turner and others. He taught his son, Edward William, to be a painter and the latter, at an early age, made drawings for the* Encyclopedia of Plants *(1820). In 1829 he stopped drawing and by 1833 Loddiges gave up the magazine, probably because he could not find a good replacement. Cooke died in 1834.*

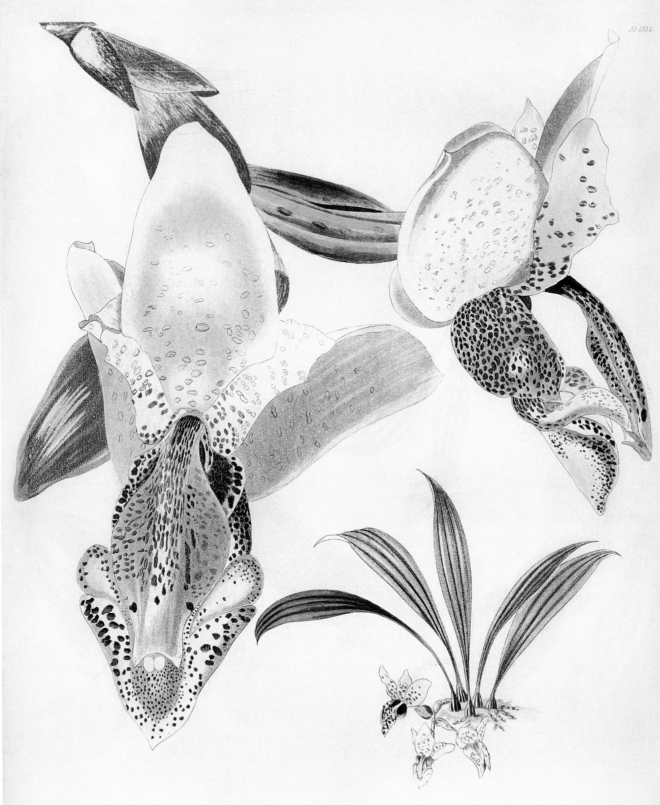

P. Loddiges. del.

Stanhopea insignis

# TRICHOPILIA CRISPA MARGINATA

Robert Warner and Benjamin S. Williams, *Select Orchidaceous Plants*

Artist: James Andrews

This is one of the handsomest of the genus and sometimes confused with *T. tortilis* but has longer and narrower leaves. Josef Warscewicz discovered it in Central America in 1849 and the plant slowly became introduced into European collections. With small flowers, to about four inches, and not as glamorous as the large cattleyas and laelias, it did not receive much attention until the twentieth century when it was rediscovered by American hobbyists and became quite popular.

The flowers are finely etched in red and the sometimes twisted petals, usually pink, form a contrasting background for the flowers. The flowers that last for weeks bloom from the base and there may be many to a plant. In its original habitat it was considered a weed rather than an exotic plant.

H. G. Reichenbach designated the plant Trichopilia, departing from John Lindley who at one time included it in the genus Helcia.

Trichopilia crispa marginata

# VANDA COERULEA

Sydenham Edwards, *The Botanical Register: Illustrations of Orchidaceous Plants*
Artist: Miss C. Sowerby

This orchid is one of my favorites because it was the first orchid I cultivated when living in Chicago, Illinois in the 1970s. The pale blue flowers were striking and today thirty years later we have many hybrids that are true blue, almost violet in color. It was found in the Khasi Hills in India at an altitude of 5,000 feet by William Griffith in 1837 and the *Botanical Register* featured it in 1847. Three years later it was rediscovered by J. D. Hooker in his *Himalayan Journals*. The first plants to blossom were exhibited at the meeting of the Horticultural Society of London in 1850. Because of its blue color, unique in the orchid world, it was given tremendous publicity and appeared in countless journals from Van Houtte's *Fleurs des Serres* and Joseph Paxton's *Flower Garden*, to Linden's publications, Warner's *The Orchid Album*, and many others.

So many collectors sought it out that there are numerous places where it was said to be found. However it was and is considered a mountainous plant growing at high altitudes and requiring cool temperatures to bloom well.

*Charlotte Caroline Sowerby 1820–65*

*The Sowerby family was composed of artists and naturalists; James was perhaps the most famous member, but Charlotte and her sister Ellen received little recognition for their work. Charlotte contributed to Henderson's* Illustrated Bouquet *and other works. Her drawings show fine talent, but she was almost completely overshadowed by the male members of the family.*

# VANDA INSIGNIS

Robert Warner and Benjamin S. Williams, *Selected Orchidaceous Plants*

Artist: W. H. Fitch

Some time prior to 1848 K. L. Blume found this orchid in parts of Java (Timor). It was rediscovered by James Veitch in 1866 and it flowered for the first time at Veitch's Chelsea nursery two years later. Although an exquisite flowering plant it was rarely grown either because importation was low or the public was not impressed by its straggling habit. To add to its confused heritage it was also supposedly discovered by William Curtis and named *V. schroederiana*. The problem with *V. insignis* is that within its form there are various color variations so classification at nurseries is not always perfect. Either way it is a beautiful orchid.

The plant generally flowers in summer with several fine four-inch flowers on pendant stems. Leaves are thick and heavy and the stem is borne from the leaf axils. It can grow quite tall in good light and with plenty of water.

The genus name vanda is derived from the Sanskrit, the ancient and sacred language of the Hindus.

Vanda insignis

# ZYGOPETALUM MACKAYI

Joseph Paxton, *Magazine of Botany*

Artist: F. W. Smith

It would be difficult to find a more colorful and exotic orchid than *Z. mackayi*. The plant was introduced by Mr. Mackay of Trinity College Botanic Garden in Dublin in about 1827 and caused a sensation in orchid circles because of its dark violet colors. It is originally from Brazil and today is a favorite among hobbyists because of its color and winter bloom time. Unlike the more plentiful cattleyas at the time this orchid hardly resembled the form we know as an orchid and much speculation took place as to just what class of plant it belongs to.

*Z. mackayi* is not easy to grow and requires a shady place and rather cool (58° F) conditions. The regal flowers are held on erect stems and pose a beautiful picture. Many varieties exist including *Z. crinitum,* which is sometimes confused with *Z. mackayi.*

The flowers have an intoxicating fragrance superior to any rose.

*Frederick W. Smith 1797–1835*

*Smith was the son of a miniaturist painter Anker Smith and brother of Edward Dalton Smith who contributed illustrations to Maund's* Botanic Garden *(vols. 1–6). Smith was a writer, talented botanical artist, and illustrated Paxton's* Magazine of Botany *(1834–37) along with Samuel Holden. He also worked for the* Floral Magazine *(1835–36) and Sweet's* British Flower Garden. *He was a consummate artist and had a talent for flowers, depicting them with accuracy. Yet his contributions to botanical art are seldom mentioned in botanical art books.*

# ORCHID PUBLICATIONS

The following are a personal selection of orchid books from my library with notes about their publishing history. As this is not an academic book I prefer to give sources here in the appendix, rather than as footnotes.

## Books

*A Century of Indian Orchids* (1895) Joseph Dalton Hooker (artist: J. D. Daas).

Some of these plates were done by Hooker himself and consist of 101 partly colored specimens. Other drawings are by Indian artists and accumulated by Hooker.

*A Second Century of Orchidaceous Plants* (1867) James Bateman.

This has one hundred fine plates by Walter Hood Fitch and one can hardly say anything derogatory about this artist's fine work. This was sequel to *A Century of Orchidaceous Plants* published by William Jackson Hooker in 1819.

*Collection des Orchidées les Plus Remarquables de l'Archipel Indien et du Japon* (1858–59) K. L. Blume.

Seventy plates, most by Wendel, engraved by G. Severyns. This is an attractive work on the orchids of the Malay district, sometimes issued under the title *Flora Javae*. Orchids are superbly handled in this book and the life size format makes the flowers even more impressive.

*Exotic Botany* (1804–05) Sir James Edward Smith.

Two volumes and 120 hand-colored plates by James Sowerby. There are several fine orchid portraits in this rare volume, noteworthy because it shows how fine an artist James Sowerby was. Smith was the foremost English botanist and founder of the Linnean Society. The unusual feature of this book is that the orchids were from the personal collections of the artist James Sowerby and Smith himself.

*Exotic Flora.* Sir William Jackson Hooker.

This fine volume shows 233 hand-colored plates by Swan and includes many fine orchid illustrations, some quite outstanding in detail and color.

*Iconographie des Orchidées d'Europe et du Basin Méditerranean* (1921) Edmund Gustave Camus.

I have only the atlas of plates with 10 colored specimens. Quite a lovely work but the orchids are not as detailed as in Bateman's or Warner's books.

*Favourite Flowers of Garden and Greenhouse* (1897) Edward Step, edited by William Watson, Assistant Curator, Kew.

Illustrated with 316 colored plates selected and arranged by G. Bois associated with the Museum Naturelle de Paris and taken from George Bois' *Atlas de Plantes de Jardin…*
This volume contains some chromolithographed drawings of many plants and includes several orchids and some hand-colored. The artist was probably B. Herincq and it can only be assumed they were taken from Bois' work.

*Illustration of Orchid Plants* (1857) Thomas Moore.

These plates are chiefly selected from *The Botanical Register.* One hundred very fine hand-colored plates much better than Moore was ever credited with, and very desirable because Moore had a great flair for design and decoration. One of my favorites.

*Orchidaceae of Mexico and Guatemala* (1837–43) James Bateman.

This is considered one, if not the best, of the color orchid volumes; its weight and size alone make it a distinctive book being elephant folio and weighting some fifteen pounds. It was called the "librarian's nightmare". However it contains some of the finest orchid drawings ever executed mainly by Miss Withers and S. A. Drake.

*Orchids and How to Grow Them in India* (1875) Samuel Jennings.

This book by Samuel Jennings is very scarce and I have only seen one copy in 35 years. It is really a fine publication and has some extraordinary drawings by F.W. Burbridge, hand-colored colored and very decorative. While the title espouses India, the orchids are mainly from all over the world.

*Orchids of the Cape Peninsula* (1893–1913) H. Bolus.

In three volumes, this seldom-seen work includes some very detailed orchid drawings by H. Bolus. The process of color printing is not outstanding and plates appear faded, but the appearance of many South African orchids make it a worthwhile inclusion.

*Orchids: The Royal Family of Plants* (1889) Harriet Stewart Miner.

Twenty-four chromolithograph drawings by Harriet Miner. These are considered quite well done but the printing process creates some inferior work hardly equal to others in the genre. While the flowers are depicted with care, the design seems crowded and the chromolith colors (in my copy) rather dull.

*Reichenbachia; Orchids Illustrated and Described* (1886–88 and 1894) Frederick Sander.

Called the Orchid King, Frederick Sander published this four-volume masterpiece with drawings by H. G. Moon, W. H. Fitch, and others. It is a monumental effort of 192 plates. Sander, at the time, was a nurseryman who was

determined to give the public a really fine orchid book with life-size depictions of the world's most famous orchids. The orchids have the elegance of Moon's flair for plants (who also made *Flora Sylva*) and the printing was superb, with hand-cut blocks made of wood and many inks used in the chromolithographs. The orchids are placed against mauve backgrounds which brings out the color of the flowers to great advantage. This magnificent book purposely issued to combat the many many orchid florilegiums was named in honor of Henry G. Reichenbach (1824–89), ornithologist, botanist, and orchidologist. His life was devoted to orchids. (My copy consists of left-over plates done on stone from an anonymous source said to have been left in a basement and never published.)

*Select Orchidaceous Plants* (1862–65) Robert Warner and B.S. Williams.

This is sometimes classed as a periodical but is really a portfolio of size. Equally impressive was Warner's *The Orchid Album* in 1882–97 with its considerable fine orchid portraits by W.H. Fitch and James Andrews.

*Sertum Orchidaceae: Wreath of the Most Beautiful Orchidaceous Flowers* (1837–41) John Lindley.

The fifty hand-colored lithographic plates are engraved by M. Gauci, mostly from Miss Drake's work. John Lindley at an early age learned botany from his father who was an inveterate nurseryman and buyer of plants for his company. Lindley met Hooker and he introduced him to Sir Joseph Banks who put him to work as a librarian. Lindley also traveled in a circle of horticulturists. He produced a work on digitalis with Ferdinand Bauer, the artist. Lindley was a perfectionist and employed the best printers to do his work.

*Select Orchidaceous Plants* (1862) Robert Warner and Benjamin Williams.

Two volumes with seventy-nine hand-colored lithos after James Andrews and Walter H. Fitch. There were several series done between 1862 and 1865 which contained forty very fine plates by two of the finest artists of the time. This volume was so successful that there was a second volume series done between 1877 and 1891. A third series was announced but I am unaware of that volume ever being produced.

*The Flower Garden* (1882–84) Joseph Paxton and John Lindley.

Joseph Paxton was a busy gardener and creator of the famous Crystal Palace greenhouse. He devised excellent ways of treating orchids properly and grew them successfully. The plates in this volume are by Walter H. Fitch and are of the finest quality as was his trademark. It is a three-volume publication.

## Periodicals

*Lindenia: Iconographie des Orchidées* (1891–97) Lucien Linden and Jean Jules Linden.

Jean Jules Linden and his younger brother Lucien produced thirteen volumes with 312 plates of incredible beauty, chromolithographed by P. de Pannemaeker and G. Severeyns from A. Goosens' drawings. (There is also a seventeen-volume 813-plate set produced between 1885 and 1901). Though the orchid plates are exquisitely detailed the colors are not as vibrant as former books which used aquatint or stipple engraving and were colored by hand. It is still magnificent to see.

*Curtis's Botanical Magazine* (1787–).

The history of this famous periodical is well documented in many orchid books. William Curtis started the magazine in 1787 as *The Botanical Magazine* to answer the demand for cultural information on exotic plants. William's son-in-law, Samuel Curtis took over from 1801 to 1845. Ownership then went to Lovell and Reeves until 1920. In 1921 the copyright was awarded to the Royal Horticultural Society and in 1984 it was taken over by The Royal Botanic Garden and incorporated into a new publication called *The Kew Magazine*. In 1994 it reverted to its original, historical name. Editors included John Sims (1800–26), William Jackson Hooker (1827–65), and Joseph Dalton Hooker (1865–1904). Most of the early plates are by Sydenham Edwards and other artists such as W. H. Fitch, James

Sowerby, and W. H. Hooker. The fine plates were hand-colored until 1984. All in all, it is a remarkable record of exotic plants including hundreds of orchids.

*The Botanical Cabinet* (1817–33) Conrad Loddiges.

This periodical featured plants from all over the world especially exotic species and contained many beautiful orchid illustrations by George Cooke after drawings by several artists. It concentrates on the early orchids. Loddiges was a nurseryman and his interest in orchids was well established. The periodical consisted of twenty volumes and was issued both in colored and partially colored editions. My edition is the latter.

*The Botanical Register* (1815–47) Sydenham Edwards.

Although he was artist for *Curtis's Botanical Magazine* for twenty-seven years, Edwards finally decided to start his own rival publication, *The Botanical Register* in 1815. The plates are by Edwards and shows his fine hand at orchids; the text for later volumes was done by John Lindley. Some thirty-three volumes were produced.

*The Botanist* and *The Botanic Garden*   Benjamin Maund.

Started by Benjamin Maund these were separate publications famous in their day for their exquisite portrayal of all kinds of flowers and employing a host of talented artists including S. A. Drake, Augusta Withers, and scores of others. *The Botanist* is perhaps the better of the two publications having full-page illustrations while *The Botanic Garden* has four flowers to a plate and many were done by the Maund sisters among other artists.

*The Floral Cabinet* Knowles and Westcott, R. Sims.

This periodical was not an immediate success nor of long duration. Only three volumes were recorded from 1847 to 1850 but they contain some very fine drawings and excellent orchid illustrations by a little known artist, R. Sims, who deserves more credit than he received during his tenure.

# BIBLIOGRAPHY

Anderson, Frank J. *An Illustrated Treasury of Cultivated Flowers*, New York: Abbeville Press, 1979.

Arber, Agnes. *Herbals. Their Origin and Evolution. A Chapter in the History of Botany*. Cambridge, England: Stearns, 1912; reprinted 1938, 1953. Third edition 1986.

Archer, Mildred. *Natural History Drawings in the India Office Library*. London: published for the Commonwealth Relations Office, 1962.

Barber, Lynn. *The Heyday of Natural History*. New York: Doubleday, 1980.

Biddle, Moncuse. *A Christmas Letter*. Philadelphia: Biddle & Co., 1945.

Blunt, Wilfrid. *The Art of Botanical Illustration*. London: Collins, 1950.

—. *Tulipmania*. Harmondsworth, England: Penguin Books, 1957.

Boyle, Frederick. *The Woodland's Orchids*. London/New York: MacMillan & Co., 1901.

Bridson, Gavin D. A., Donald E. Wendel, and James J. White. *Printmaking in the Service of Botany*. Pitsburgh: Hunt Institute for Botanical Documentation, 1986.

Buchanan, Handasyde. *Nature into Art*. London: Weidenfield and Nicolson, 1979.

Butler, June. *Floralia*. Chapel Hill: University of North Carolina Press, 1938.

Calmann, Gerta. *Ehret: Flower Painter Extraordinary: An Illustrated Biography*. Oxford: Phaidon, 1977.

*Captain Cook's Florilegium*. London: Lion and Unicorn Press, 1973.

Catlow, Agnes. *Popular Field Botany*, 3rd ed. London: Reeve and Co., 1852.

Coates, Petra. *Flowers in History*. London: Weidenfield and Nicolson, 1970.

Coats, Alice M. *Flowers and Their Histories*. London: Hutton, 1956.

—. *The Book of Flowers*. New York: McGraw-Hill, 1973.

—. *The Treasury of Flowers*. New York: McGraw-Hill, 1975.

Desmond, R. *A Celebration of Flowers: 200 Years of Curtis's Botanical Magazine*. London: Kew and Twickenham, 1992.

—. *Dictionary of Irish and British Botanists and Horticulturists and Botanical Artists*. London: Taylor & Francis, 1994.

Dunthorne, Gordon. *Flower and Fruit Prints of the 18th and Early 19th Centuries*. Washington, D.C.: 1938.

Dykes, W.R. *Notes on Tulip Species*. London: Herbert Jenkins, 1930.

Elliot, Brent. *The Treasures of the Royal Horticultural Society*. London: Hobart Press, 1994.

Fennell, James. *Drawing Room Botany*. London: Joseph Thomas, 1840.

Gage, A.T., and W.T. Stearn. *A Bicentenary History of the Linnean Society of London*. London: Academic Press, 1988.

Grandville, J.J. *The Court of Flora*. New York: Braziller, 1981.

Griegson, Mary. *An English Florilegium*. New York: Abbeville Press, 1988.

Hadfield, Miles, Robert Harling, and Leonie Highton. *British Gardeners: A Biographical Dictionary*. London: Zwemmer, 1980.

Henrey, Blanche. *British Botanical and Horticultural Literature Before 1800*. 3 vols. London: Oxford University Press, 1975.

Hepper, F. Nigel (ed.). *Kew, Gardens for Science and Pleasure*. Owings Mills, MD: Stemmer House, 1982.

L'Heritier. *Sertum Anglicum* (facsimile). George Lawrence Edition. Pittsburgh: Hunt Institute for Botanical Documentation, 1963.

Hey, Mrs. *The Moral of Flowers*. London: Longman, 1849.

Hulme, Edward F. *Flower Painting in Water Colours*. London: Cassell Petter Galpin, n.d.

Hulton, Paul, and Lawrence Smith. *Flowers in Art from East and West*. London: British Museum Publications, 1979.

Jardine, Sir William. *The Naturalist's Library*, vol. XI, by James Duncan. London: 1843.

Kaden, Vero. *The Illustration of Plants and Gardens 1500–1850*. London: Victoria and Albert Museum, n.d.

Kramer, Jack. *Growing Orchids at Your Windows*. Van Nostrand, 1968.

—. *Rare Orchids Everyone Can Grow*, 1970.

—. *The World Wildlife Fund Book of Orchids*. New York; Abbeville, 1989.

—. *Women of Flowers*. New York: STC, 1996.

—. *Orchids for the South*, 1996.

—. *Growing Orchids Indoors*, 1999.

Lewis, Jan. *Walter Hood Fitch*. London: HMSO, 1992.

Leonard, Elizabeth. *Painting Flowers*. Watson Guptill, 1986.

Lindbert, Jana Hauschild. *Orchids and Exotic Flowers*. New York: Dover, 1986.

Mabey, Richard. *The Frampton Flora*. Englewood Cliffs, NJ: Prentice-Hall, 1989.

—. *The Flowers of Kew*. New York: Atheneum, 1989.

Marshal, Alexander. *Mr. Marshal's Flower Album, from the Royal Library at Windsor Castle*. London: Gollancz, 1985.

McIntosh, Charles. *The Flower Garden*. London: William Orr, 1838.

—. *The Greenhouse*. London: William Orr, 1840.

—. *The New and Improved Practical Gardener*. London: Thomas Kelly, 1860.

McTigue, Bernard. *Nature Illustrated*. New York: Abrams, 1989.

Metropolitan Museum of Art. *Metropolitan Flowers*. New York: Abrams, 1982.

*Mille et un Livres Botaniques de la Collection Arpad Plesch*. Brussels, Belgium: Arcade Publishing, 1973.

Nissen, Claus. *Die Botanische Buchillustration*. Stuggart: Anton Hiersemann, 1966.

Pritzel, G.A. *Theasaurus Literaturae Botanicae*. Leipzig: 1872.

*A Redouté Treasury*. London: Vendome Press, 1989.

Reinikka, M. *A History of the Orchid*. Coral Gables, Fl: University of Miami Press, 1972.

Renneville, Rene Augustin Constantin de. *A Collection of Voyages Undertaken by the Dutch East-India Company*. London: 1703.

Rix, Martyn. *The Art of the Plant World*. Woodstock, NY: Overlook Press, 1979.

Ross-Craig, Stella. *Drawings of British Plants*. London: Bell & Sons, 1950.

Seaton, Beverly. *Language of Flowers*. University of Virginia, 1995.

Scourse, Nicolette. *The Victorians and Their Flowers*. Portland, OR: Timber Press, 1983.

Sitwell, Sacheverelle, and Wilfrid Blunt. *Great Flower Books 1700–1900*. London: Collins, 1956.

Smith, Bernard. *European Visions and the South Pacific 1786–1850*. London: Oxford University Press, 1960.

*Sotheby's Magnificent Botanical Book* (florilegium). London: Sotheby's, 1987.

Stearn, William Thomas. *The Australian Flower Paintings of Ferdinand Bauer*. Lonodn: Basilisk Press, 1976.

—. *Flower Artists of Kew*. London: Herbert Press, 1990.

*Stiftung für Botanik Library*, 3 parts. London: Sotheby's, 1975.

Swinson, Arthur. *Frederick Sanders, the Orchid King*. London: Hodder and Stoughton, 1970.

Symonds, Mrs. John Addington. *Recollections of a Happy Life … Marianne North*, 2 vols. New York: MacMillan, 1893.

Synge, P. M. *R. H. S. Dictionary of Gardening*. London: Oxford University Press, 1956.

Da Vinci, Leonardo. *Selected Drawings from Windsor Castle: Leonardo da Vinci*. London: Phaidon, 1954.

Walpole, Michael. *Natural History Illustration, 1485–1968*. Loughborough Technical College, 1969.

Whittle, Tyler. *The Plant Hunters*. Chilton Books, 1970.

Wilkinson, Lady. *Weeds and Wild Flowers*. London: John Van Voorst, 1858.

Wirt, Mrs. E. W. *Flora's Dictionary*. Baltimore: Lucas Bros., 1855.

Wunderlich, Eleanor. *Botanical Illustrations in Watercolor*. Watson Guptill, 1991.

## Catalogs

*The Art of Botanical Illustration*. Bryn Mawr, PA: Bryn Mawr College Library, 1973.

*Catalogue of the Natural History Drawings*. Commissioned by Joseph Banks on the Endeavour Voyage 1768–1771. Westport, CT: Meckler Publishing in association with British Museum, 1984–86.

Garden Club of America. *Plant Illustration Before 1850*. New York: The Grolier Club, 1941.

Getscher, Dr. Robert H. *A Garden of Prints*. Cincinnati: Fine Arts Gallery, John Carroll University, 1980.

Grant, M. H. *Flower Painting Through Four Centuries: A Descriptive Catalogue of the Collection Formed by Major the Honorable Henry Rogers Broughton*. Leigh-on-Sea, Essex, England: nd.

Holmgren, Noel H., and Bobbi Angell. *Botanical Illustrations: Preparation for Publication*. New York: New York Botanical Garden, 1986.

Hunt Institute for Botanical Documentation. *The Hunt Botanical Catalogue*, vol. 1, "Printed Books 1477–1700", compiled by Jane Quimby; vol. 2, part 1, "Printed Books 1701–1800", part 2, "Introduction to Printed Books 1701–1800", compiled by Allan Stephenson. Pittsburgh: 1958 (vol. 1), 1961 (vol. 2).

—. *A Catalogue of Redouteana*. Pittsburgh, 1963.

—. *Catalogue of an Exhibition of Contemporary Botanical Art and Illustration*, April 6 to September 1, 1964. Pittsburgh: 1964.

—. *A Selection of Twentieth Century Botanical Art and Illustration*; Compiled by George H. M. Lawrence.

Pittsburgh: XI International Botanical Congress, 1969.

—. *Biographical Dictionary of Botanists Represented in the Hunt Institute Portrait Collection.* Boston: Hall, 1972.

—. *Artists from the Royal Botanic Gardens, Kew, by Gilbert Daniels.* Pittsburgh: 1974.

—. *Fourth International Exhibition of Botanical Art and Illustration,* Nov. 6, 1977–Mar. 31., 1978. Compiled by Sally W. Secrist and N. Ann Howard; Introduction by John V. Brindle. Pittsburgh: 1977.

—. White, James Joseph. *Fifth International Exhibition of Botanical Art and Illustration,* Apr. 11–July 15, 1983. Pittsburgh: 1983.

—. Brindle, John V., and James White. *Flora Portrayed.* Pittsburgh: 1985.

Milwaukee Art Museum. *Focus, The Flower in Art.* Milwaukee: 1986.

Pierpont Morgan Library. *Flowers in Book and Drawings c. 940–1840.* New York: 1980.

Washington International Exhibitions Foundation. Scrase, David. *Flowers of Three Centuries. One Hundred Drawings and Watercolors from the Broughton Collection.* Introduction by Michael Jaffé. 1983–84.

## Exhibitions

*Plant Illustrations Before 1850*
The Garden Club of America of the Grolier Club, New York 1941.

*The Art of Botanical Illustrations*
Exhibition from the Botany Collection of the Library of Victoria 1975.

*Fower Books and Drawings, c. 940–1840*
The Pierpont Morgan Library, New York 1983–84.

*Flower Books and Their Illustrators*
Wilfred Blunt, An Exhibition arranged for the National Book League, Cambridge University Press.

*Botanical Books, Prints, and Drawings*
From the Collection of Mrs. Roy Arthur Hunt, Dept. of Fine Arts, Carnegie Institute, Pittsburgh 1952.

*Natural History Illustration 1458–1968*
Loughborough Technical College (Collection from Michael Walpole held at the School of Librarianships, March 1969).

*A Garden of Prints*
An exhibition of eighteenth and nineteenth century botanical illustrators. Sponsored by Vixebixse Art Galleries and John Carroll University. Catalogue by Dr. Robert Getschler, Fine Arts Gallery, 1980.

*Flowers of Three Centuries*
One-hundred drawings and watercolors from the Broughton Collection, by David Scrase, International Exhibition Foundation, Washington, D.C. Shown at the Pierpont Morgan Library.

*An Oak Spring Garland*
Illustrated Books, Prints, Drawings, from the Oak Spring Garden Library, Upperville, Virginia 1989. Described by Sandra Raphael.

*The Orchid Observed, Five Centuries of Botanical Illustration*
An exhibition of books from the collection of William Glikberg and the Stanford Universities Libraries, Stanford, CA, 1982–83.

Following is a selection of the many institutions that have collections of botanical art:

## United States
Pierpont Morgan Library, New York
Library of Congress, Washington, D.C.
Arnold Arboretum
Brooklyn Botanic Gardens (Library)
Missouri Botanic Gardens, St. Louis
Massachusetts Horticultural Society, Boston
Pennsylvania Horticultural Society, Philadelphia

## England
Fitzwilliam Museum, Cambridge
Royal Botanic Gardens, Kew, Richmond
The Bodleian Library, Oxford
The Linnean Society of London
British Museum, London
Victoria and Albert Museum, London

## Printing Techniques

Today, an original drawing signifies a treatment by one person in—oils, watercolors, etc. But in earlier centuries, several artists were involved in producing a replica.

### Woodblocking

The woodblock was the most popular and was used extensively in the fifteenth and sixteenth centuries. An image was carved into wood, ink was applied to the raised ridges, and the inked ridges made contact with the paper during printing. The artist drew the image; the craftsman transferred the image onto wood; the woodcutter cut the block. The illustration, after being printed via contact with paper, was then colored by hand.

### Engravings/Etchings

In engraving, the images are cut into the surface of a metal plate or block. The lines are thus below the surface.

Generally, a sheet of copper that has been smoothed and polished is used. The types of lines made determine the final image: cross-hatching creates a heavy line; closely cut light lines produce light shading.

In an etched plate, the sunken lines are burned into the plate with acid. A simple needle-nosed instrument is used to draw the image; when the drawing is completed, the lines shine through the wax or varnish. The plate is immersed in a bath of dilute nitric acid, which "bites" into the plate. Finally, the varnish is removed with turpentine. The length of time the plate is in the acid determines the depth of the lines; variation in depth creates the tone.

An engraver or a good colorist can make an ordinary plate outstanding. Color is applied by hand.

The mezzotinting process did not satisfy the demand for decorative floral art. Thus the stipple engraving and aquatint processes evolved. They produced subtle gradations of tone rather than line and were the missing link between a fine drawing and an extraordinary one. Stipple engraving had been used in France but not for floral drawings. The process itself is an extension of the etching method, but dots that are made with a tool called a roulette rather than lines made with needles are bitten into the surface of the plate with acid.

The stipple-engraved plate yields an almost perfect portrait. In some cases, after the plate was made, hand coloring with watercolor washes was still done with a brush.

Aquatint, another process of doing floral plates, was commonly used in Italy and England. A copper plate is dusted with a powdered resin and the plate is then heated. When the plate cools, the resin coating adheres to the surface. The image is drawn on this surface; acid bites the areas of varying depths into the plate. During printing, the bitten areas hold the ink.

### Lithography

Printing from a stone (lithography) was discovered by Aloys Senefelder in Germany in 1797. Supposedly Senefelder had used up his paper supply and so put some markings on a stone he used for grinding inks and found that the ink resisted the acid he used for cleaning the stone.

The lithographic process involves grease and water. The drawing is made directly on stone or a zinc plate with a greasy crayon or ink. The drawing is affixed to the stone by washing the stone with a weak solution of gum Arabic and acid. When the stone is dampened with water and inked with a roller, the ink sticks to the greasy ink or crayon residue. With lithography, images are accurately reproduced, and subtle gradations of tone, from silvery gray to velvety black, are achieved.

Chromolithography—printing from a stone and in color—was developed when it was discovered that flat spaces on the stone could be covered. Now successive printings in different colors could be done, so it was possible to make a colored print. Because chromolithography saved so much time and expense, it was used extensively for printing botanical books in the mid-nineteenth century.

Perhaps the best example of lithography is James Bateman's *Orchidaceae of Mexico and Guatemala* (1837–43), with hand-colored drawings by Miss S.A. Drake and lithographed by Augusta Withers and M. Gauci.

Because chromolithography saved so much time it was used extensively for printing many botanical books in the mid-nineteenth century. The technique costs and production troubles were less expensive but in no way could match the beauty of the other color processes.

The late nineteenth century saw the emergence of photography in orchid books.

# INDEX OF NAMES AND ORCHIDS

Numbers in *italics* refer to illustrations